Learning About
Lincoln

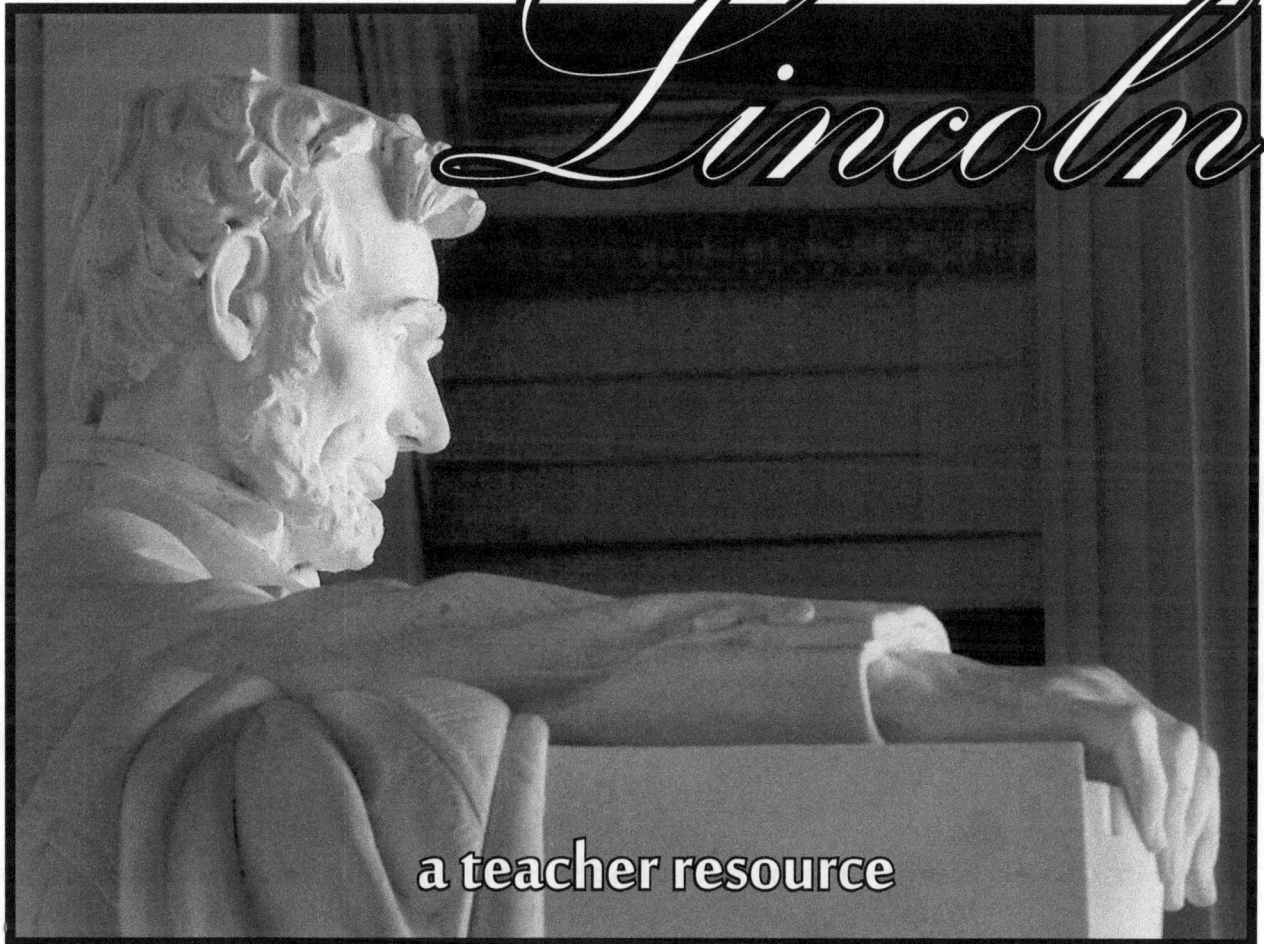

a teacher resource

Katie Fraser Carpenter

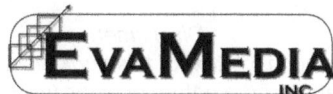

EVAMEDIA
INC

© 2009

Learning About Lincoln
A Teacher Resource

by Katie Fraser Carpenter

edited by Kate Larken

ISBN 978-1-934894-21-7

EVAMEDIA
INC

Louisville, Kentucky

www.EVAMEDIA.com

EducationTeam@EvaMedia.com

IMAGES COURTESY OF:
LINCOLN MEMORIAL UNIVERSITY – front/back covers; pages 4, 11, 12, 27, 28, 90, 99, 100
AUTHOR'S COLLECTION – pages 1, 89, 136, 137, 138, 139, 140, 141, 142
EK LARKEN – page 143

Table of Contents

LINCOLN THE LAWYER

LET EVERY AMERICAN, EVERY LOVER
OF LIBERTY, EVERY WELL WISHER TO
HIS POSTERITY, SWEAR BY THE BLOOD
OF THE REVOLUTION NEVER TO VIOLATE
IN THE LEAST PARTICULAR THE LAWS
OF THE COUNTRY

SPRINGFIELD ILL. JAN. 27. 1838

Author's Introduction

WHY DO WE ALL NEED TO KNOW ABOUT ABRAHAM LINCOLN?

We hear it all the time: Abraham Lincoln was the greatest of our presidents. Yet during his presidency, the United States fought the worst war in its history – in terms of loss of the life, the destruction, and the deep regional hatred it engendered.

Mr. Lincoln freed the slaves and saved the Union. But the Emancipation Proclamation was a wartime measure; it only freed slaves in the Confederate states. And, to save the Union, was all the horror of the Civil War necessary?

What matters is the kind of Union Mr. Lincoln was able to save. A man of deep and abiding principle, he wanted to save a particular kind of Union – a Union that was dedicated to the proposition that all people are created equal. In truth, it hadn't been that way, not since the Declaration of Independence in 1776, because one-sixth of its population was enslaved to the majority.

Some argue that the U.S. Civil War was not about slavery, that it was about the deep economic divide between North and South, or the fact that the Southerners perceived themselves culturally and socially distinct from the North. For many Southerners, the war was about states' rights; they called it "The War of Northern Aggression." But for Mr. Lincoln, it was about slavery – slavery was inherently evil and it was preventing the United States from being a true beacon of hope for oppressed peoples everywhere. It is for this reason that we celebrate his birth and his legacy to us: a truly good man, a man of principle and honor who believed that what was right was worth fighting for. The fact that he succeeded is one of the greatest achievements in human history.

The more we think about Mr. Lincoln and try to understand him and his times, the more we realize we, as Americans, have much to be grateful for and much to celebrate.

ABOUT THIS BOOK

This book, intended for the classroom teacher in grades 4-8, offers activities and resources for teaching about Abraham Lincoln, borrowing techniques from the Arts & Humanities curriculum to engage students' imaginations and to motivate them to want to learn more about the 16th U.S. President. The material concentrates on fostering deep understanding through application and synthesis, rather than simple memorization of salient facts.

An extensive list of resources includes interactive websites, images, places to visit and artifacts because all teachers know that students understand more when they can touch and feel and experience, rather than simply read a book or watch a movie. However, a number of excellent literary and screen resources are included as well.

Because Abraham Lincoln was born in Kentucky, spent much of his boyhood in Indiana, and built his political career in Illinois, activities have been created with those states' academic criteria in mind; however, Learning About Lincoln is suitable for use with any state's (or national) standards of learning.

Targeted Academic Content

KENTUCKY

The primary Core Content addressed in this resource book is for Social Studies and Arts & Humanities. Lessons engage students' attention and deepen their understanding of Core Content, rather than serving only as an introduction or summary. Connections are most clearly made to the following:

Intermediate Grades (Grades 4-5)

SOCIAL STUDIES

Formation of Governments
SS-04/05-1.1.1; SS-04/05.1.1.2; SS-04-1.2.1; SS-04-1.2.2; SS-04/05-1.3.1; SS-04.1.3.2
Understanding why President Lincoln believed the Civil War was necessary helps young students understand the significance of the Constitution and the Declaration of Independence. President Lincoln believed the Civil War was necessary to keep the Union together and abolish slavery so that the principles for which we separated from England (e.g., life, liberty, and the pursuit of happiness) could be honored.

Cultures and Societies
SS-04/05-2.1.1; SS-04/05-2.2.1; SS-04/05-2.3.1; SS-04/05-2.3.2
The story of Abraham Lincoln's experiences growing up on the Kentucky and Indiana frontiers is a microcosm of what happened to the state and the country.

Economics
SS-04/05-3.1.1
Scarcity affected the economic choices of pioneer families such as Lincoln's and also played a major role in the development of the country in the first half of the 19th Century. Understanding Mr. Lincoln's life involves understanding the production, distribution, and consumption of goods and services in the history of the U.S. and the state, as well as how new knowledge, technology/tools and specialization increased productivity.

Geography
SS-04/05-4.1.1; SS-04/05-4.1.2; SS-04/05-4.1.3; SS-04/05-4.3.1; SS-04/05-4.4.1; SS-04/05.4.4.2
An understanding of the physical location is essential to understanding Mr. Lincoln's experiences growing up, especially in how his family adapted the environment for their own needs. The development of the country in the first half of the 19th Century into slave-owning and non-slave-owning sections is dictated by geography.

Historical Perspective
SS-04/05-5.1.1; SS-04/05-5.2.1; SS-04/05-5.2.2; SS-05-5.2.4
Students use a variety of primary and secondary sources to investigate Mr. Lincoln's life and legacy. Mr. Lincoln was deeply involved in incidents and issues in the United States up through 1865; his lasting effect on the country is still recognized in our own time.

ARTS & HUMANITIES

Structures in the Arts
MUSIC: AH-04/05-1.1.1 (elements of music); AH-04/05-1.1.2 (styles of music); DRAMA/THEATRE: AH-04/05-1.3.1 (elements of drama); AH-04/05-1.3.2 (character relationships); AH-04/05-1.3.3 (creative dramatics);
VISUAL ART: AH-04/05-1.4.1 (elements of art and principles of design); AH-04/05-1.4.2 (media and processes)

Humanity in the Arts
MUSIC: AH-04/05-2.1.1 (Music in colonial America and Appalachia; European influence)

Purposes for Creating the Arts
MUSIC: AH-04/05.3.1.1 (purposes of music); DRAMA/THEATRE: AH-04/05-3.3.1 (purposes of drama/theater); VISUAL ART: AH-04/05-3.4.1 (purposes of visual art)

Processes in the Arts
DRAMA/THEATRE: AH-04/05-4.3.1 (creating and performing drama); AH-04/05-4.4.3.2 (storytelling); VISUAL ART: AH-04/05-4.4.1 (creating artwork); AH-04/05-4.4.2 (using a variety of media and processes)

Middle School (Grades 6-8)

SOCIAL STUDIES

Formation of Governments
SS-06/07/08-1.1.1; SS-08.1.1.2; SS-08-1.2.1; SS-08-1.2.2; SS-08-1.3.1; SS-08-1.3.2
An understanding of the Constitution and the Declaration of Independence is essential if students are to understand the causes of the Civil War.

Cultures and Societies
SS-08-2.2.1; SS-08-2.3.1; SS-08-2.3.2
Abraham Lincoln's experiences in Kentucky and Indiana stand as an example of how the western territories were settled.

Economics
SS-08-3.1.1; SS-08-3.1.2; SS-08-3.2.1; SS-08-3.2.2; SS-08-3.4.1; SS-08-3.4.2; SS-08-3.4.3
Scarcity affected the economic choices of pioneer families such as Lincoln's and also played a major role in the development of the country in the first half of the 19th Century. Understanding Mr. Lincoln's life involves understanding the production, distribution, and consumption of goods and services in the history of the U.S. and the state, as well as how new knowledge, technology/tools and specialization increased productivity.

Geography
SS-06/07/08-4.1.1; SS-08-4.1.2; SS-06/08-4.2.1; SS-06/08-4.2.2; SS-08-4.3.1; SS-08.4.3.2
An understanding of physical location is essential to understanding Mr. Lincoln's experiences growing up, especially in how his family adapted the environment for their own needs. The development of the country in the first half of the 19th Century into slave-owning and non-slave-owning sections is dictated by geography.

Historical Perspective
SS-04/05-5.1.1; SS-04/05-5.2.1; SS-04/05-5.2.2; SS-05-5.2.4
Students use a variety of primary and secondary sources to investigate Mr. Lincoln's life and legacy. Mr. Lincoln was deeply involved in the incidents and issues in the United States up through 1865; and he has had a lasting effect on the country still recognized in our own time.

ARTS & HUMANITIES

Structures in the Arts
MUSIC: AH-06/07/08-1.1.1 (elements of music); DRAMA/THEATRE: AH-06/07/08-1.3.1 (elements of drama); AH-04/05-1.3.2 (technical elements); AH-06/07/08-1.3.3 (performance elements); VISUAL ART: AH-06/07/08-1.4.1 (elements of art and principles of design); AH-06/07/08-1.4.2 (media and processes)

Humanity in the Arts
MUSIC: AH-08-2.1.1 (diverse cultures – early America through Civil War); VISUAL ART AH-08-2.4.1 (diverse cultures – photography)

Purposes for Creating the Arts
MUSIC: AH-06/07/08.3.1.1 (purposes of music); DRAMA/THEATRE: AH-06/07/08-3.3.1 (purposes of drama/theater); VISUAL ART: AH-06/07/08-3.4.1 (purposes of visual art)

Processes in the Arts
MUSIC AH-06/07/08 (creative music); DRAMA/THEATRE: AH-06/07/08-4.3.1/2/3/4 (creating and performing drama); AH-04/05-4.4.3.2 (storytelling); VISUAL ART: AH-04/05-4.4.1 (creating artwork); AH-06/07/08-4.4.1/2 (using a variety of media and processes)

Targeted Academic Content
<u>INDIANA</u>

Social Studies

FOURTH GRADE
Students in Grade 4 study Indiana and its relationships to regional, national and world communities, including the influence of physical and cultural environments on the state's growth and development and principles and practices of citizenship and government in Indiana.

Standard 1: History
Students will trace the historical periods, places, people, events and movements that have led to the development of Indiana as a state.

Standard 2: Civics and Government
Students will describe the components and characteristics of Indiana's constitutional form of government.

Standard 3: Geography
Students will describe the major physical and cultural characteristics of Indiana; give examples of how people have adapted to and modified their environment, past and present; identify regions of Indiana.

Standard 4: Economics
Students will study and compare the characteristics of Indiana's changing economy in the past and present.

FIFTH GRADE
Students in fifth grade study the United States, focusing on the influence of physical and cultural environments on national origins, growth, and development up to 1800. This background helps them understand the influence of Abraham Lincoln on the country's continuing development.

SIXTH GRADE
Students in sixth grade study the regions and countries of Europe and the Americas.

Standard 1: History
Students will explore the key historic movements, events and figures that contributed to the development of modern Europe and America from early civilizations through modern times by examining religious institutions, trade and cultural interactions, political institutions, and technological developments, especially 6.1.15, 6.1.16, 6.1.18, 6.1.19, 6.1.20, 6.1.21, 6.1.22, 6.1.23, and 6.1.24.

Standard 2: Civics and Government
Students will compare and contrast forms of government in different historical periods with contemporary political structures of Europe and the Americas and examine the rights and responsibilities of individuals in different political systems, especially 6.2.1 and 6.2.5.

Standard 4: Economics
Students will examine the influence of physical and cultural factors upon the economic systems of countries in Europe and the Americas, especially 6.4.2.

SEVENTH GRADE
Students in seventh grade study the regions and nations of Africa, Asia and the Southwest Pacific. (NOTE: Most slaves in the U.S. had been citizens or descendents of West African cultures.)

EIGHTH GRADE
In eighth grade, students focus upon United States history, beginning with a brief review of early history, including the Revolution and Founding Era, and the principles of the United States and Indiana constitutions, as well as other founding documents and their applications to subsequent periods of national history and to civic and political life. Students then study national development, westward expansion, social reform movements, and the Civil War and Reconstruction.

Standard 1: History
Students will examine the relationship and significance of themes, concepts, and movements in the development of United States history, including review of key ideas related to the colonization of America and the revolution and Founding Era. This will be followed by emphasis on social reform, national development and westward expansion, and the Civil War and Reconstruction period.

Standard 2: Civics and Government
Students will explain the major principles, values and institutions of constitutional government and citizenship, which are based on the founding documents of the United States and how three branches of government share and check power within our federal system of government.

Standard 3: Geography
Students will identify the major geographic characteristics of the United States and its regions. They will name and locate the major physical features of the United States.

Standard 4: Economics
Students will identify, describe and evaluate the influence of economic factors on national development from the founding of the nation to the end of Reconstruction.

The Arts

GRADES 4-8		
Theatre	Standard 3:	Students understand and analyze the dramatic structure of plays and performances.
	Standard 4:	Students identify, develop, and apply criteria to make informed judgments about theatre.
	Standard 5.	Students reflect on and interpret the nature of the theatre experience and its personal and artistic significance.
	Standard 6:	Students create scripts and theatre pieces through collaboration, inquiry, and improvisation.
	Standard 7:	Students utilize imagination and research to design and implement the visual environment.
	Standard 8:	Students develop acting skills through observation, improvisation, and script analysis.
Visual Arts	Standard 3:	Students describe, research, and interpret works of art and artifacts.
	Standard 4:	Students identify and apply criteria to make informed judgments about art.
	Standard 7:	Students observe, select, and utilize a range of subject matter, symbols, and ideas in their work.
	Standard 8:	Students understand and apply elements and principles of design effectively in their work.
	Standard 9:	Students develop and apply skills using a variety of two-dimensional and three dimensional media, tools, and processes to create works that communicate personal meaning.
	Standard 13:	Students identify and make connections between knowledge and skill in art and all other subject areas such as humanities, sciences, and technology.
	Standard 14:	Students understand the integrative nature of art forms including dance, theater, music, visual art, and media art.
Music	Standard 6:	Responding to music: Listening to, analyzing, and describing music.
	Standard 8:	Responding to music: Understanding relationships between music, the other arts, and disciplines outside the arts.
	Standard 9:	Responding to music: Understanding music in relation to history and culture.

Targeted Academic Content

ILLINOIS

All Grades

Language Arts

STATE GOAL 1: Read with understanding and fluency *(with respect to changing vocabulary usages over time, reading for research, content area language)*
STATE GOAL 3: Write to communicate for a variety of purposes *(with respect to demonstrating learning through research, analysis and reporting/creating)*
STATE GOAL 4: Listen and speak effectively in a variety of situations *(with respect to evaluating information, interpreting a message, or developing a presentation)*
STATE GOAL 5: Use the language arts to acquire, assess and communicate information *(with respect to both historic documents and student-created projects as a means of analyzing and demonstrating learning)*

Social Studies

STATE GOAL 14: Understand political systems, with an emphasis on the United States *(with respect to government and its responsibilities)*
STATE GOAL 15: Understand economic systems, with an emphasis on the United States *(with respect to slavery as an economic engine and, conversely, the Emancipation Proclamation as a means to limit the economy in the states that seceded from the Union during the Civil War)*
STATE GOAL 16: Understand events, trends, individuals and movements shaping the history of Illinois, the United States and other nations *(with respect to historic figures, issues and elections)*
STATE GOAL 18: Understand social systems, with an emphasis on the United States *(with respect to cultural and military factors in US history)*

Fine Arts

STATE GOAL 26: Through creating and performing, understand how works of art are produced *(with respect to problem-solving, creativity, and active hands-on learning)*
STATE GOAL 27: Understand the role of the arts in civilizations, past and present *(with respect to learning about culture and people by studying records from the past)*

Chapter One

About Mr. Lincoln

ABRAHAM LINCOLN
The Official White House Biography

Lincoln warned the South in his Inaugural Address: "In your hands, my dissatisfied fellow countrymen, and not in mine, is the momentous issue of civil war. The government will not assail you.... You have no oath registered in Heaven to destroy the government, while I shall have the most solemn one to preserve, protect and defend it."

Lincoln thought secession illegal and was willing to use force to defend federal law and the Union. When Confederate batteries fired on Fort Sumter and forced its surrender, he called on the states for 75,000 volunteers. Four more slave states joined the Confederacy, but four remained within the Union. The Civil War had begun.

The son of a Kentucky frontiersman, Lincoln always had to struggle for a living and for learning. Five months before receiving his party's nomination for President, he sketched his life:

"I was born Feb. 12, 1809, in Hardin County, Kentucky. My parents were both born in Virginia, of undistinguished families – second families, perhaps I should say. My mother, who died in my tenth year, was of a family of the name of Hanks. ...My father...removed from Kentucky to... Indiana, in my eighth year. ...It was a wild region, with many bears and other wild animals still in the woods. There I grew up. ...Of course when I came of age I did not know much. Still somehow, I could read, write, and cipher...but that was all."

Lincoln made extraordinary efforts to attain knowledge while working on a farm, splitting rails for fences, and keeping store at New Salem, Illinois. He was a captain in the Black Hawk War, spent eight years in the Illinois legislature, and rode the circuit of courts for many years. His law partner said of him, "His ambition was a little engine that knew no rest."

He married Mary Todd, and they had four boys, only one of whom lived to maturity. In 1858 Lincoln ran against Stephen A. Douglas for Senator. He lost the election, but in debating with Douglas he gained a national reputation that won him the Republican nomination for President in 1860.

As President, he built the Republican party into a strong national organization. Further, he rallied most of the northern Democrats to the Union cause. On January 1, 1863, he issued the Emancipation Proclamation that declared forever free those slaves within the Confederacy.

Lincoln never let the world forget that the Civil War involved an even larger issue. This he stated most movingly in dedicating the military cemetery at Gettysburg: "...we here highly resolve that these dead shall not have died in vain – that this nation, under God, shall have a new birth of freedom – and that government of the people, by the people, for the people, shall not perish from the earth."

Lincoln won re-election in 1864, as Union military triumphs heralded an end to the war. In his planning for peace, the President was flexible and generous, encouraging Southerners to lay down their arms and join speedily in reunion.

The spirit that guided him was clearly that of his Second Inaugural Address, now inscribed on one wall of the Lincoln Memorial in Washington, D.C.: "With malice toward none; with charity for all; with firmness in the right, as God gives us to see the right, let us strive on to finish the work we are in; to bind up the nation's wounds...."

On Good Friday, April 14, 1865, Lincoln was assassinated at Ford's Theatre in Washington by John Wilkes Booth, who somehow thought his act of murder was helping the South. In fact, the opposite occurred, for with Lincoln's death the possibility of peace with magnanimity died.

ABRAHAM LINCOLN Q & A

THE KENTUCKY YEARS

When and where was Abraham Lincoln born?

Abraham Lincoln was born February 12, 1809, on Sinking Spring Farm, in Hardin County, Kentucky. He was the first president born outside of the original 13 colonies. Kentucky had become the 15th state in 1792.

Who were his parents?

His father was Thomas Lincoln, who entered Kentucky from Virginia as a boy. Thomas' father, after whom Abraham was named, farmed land near Louisville and was killed by Indians. Like most pioneers, Thomas was a farmer as well, but he also was a highly skilled carpenter.

The future President's mother was Nancy Hanks Lincoln. She also was born in Virginia and emigrated to Kentucky as a child. Nancy died of "milk sickness" two years after the family moved to Indiana. Abraham was nine years old.

Did he have any brothers or sisters?

Abraham's sister, Sarah, was two years older. She died when she was 19, giving birth to her second child; the child died as well.

Abraham's younger brother, Thomas, died when he was a few weeks old.

Did he have any nicknames?

No. He intensely disliked the nickname "Abe." However, his name was probably pronounced more like "A'bram" than Abraham. He often signed his name as "A. Lincoln."

Where did he live as a child?

For the first two years of his life, he lived on Sinking Spring Farm, in Hardin County, Kentucky.

When he was two, the family moved a few miles away to Knob Creek Farm. The property was on the main road that led from Louisville to Nashville. Today, that highway is called 31E.

Where did he first go to school?

At the age of six and again when he was seven, Abraham Lincoln attended school for a few weeks with his sister, Sarah.

THE INDIANA YEARS

Where did Abraham Lincoln live in Indiana?

The Lincoln family moved to Indiana in 1816, when Abraham was seven, and settled in what is now Spencer County, near Lincoln City. The move was, as Mr. Lincoln said later, partly because his father had difficulty proving he owned the land in Kentucky (this happened to many early settlers) and partly because of slavery. Slavery was legal in Kentucky, but when Indiana became a state in 1816, slavery was illegal.

What happened when his mother died?

Nancy Hanks Lincoln died of "milk sickness" a year after the family moved to Indiana. The family was on its own for a year.

Sarah (Sally) Bush Johnston Lincoln became Abraham's stepmother when he was ten. His father returned to Kentucky to marry and bring her back. Abraham and Sally became very fond of each other; Abraham called her "Mother." She had three children of her own: Elizabeth, John and Matilda.

Where did he go to school in Indiana?

Parents paid for children to attend school in Indiana in the early 19th Century – rather like paying a piano teacher for lessons in the 21st Century. Sometimes a neighbor offered his services as teacher; sometimes no one was available. Abraham, along with the other children in the family, attended three different schools before he was twelve. In all, he had less than a year of formal schooling.

What were his favorite books as a boy?

Even though he had so little schooling, Abraham loved to read, and Sally owned several books (unusual for the time). His favorites were *Aesop's Fables, The Pilgrim's Progress, The Arabian Nights,* and *The Life of George Washington.*

Did he have a job as a teenager?

There was plenty of farmwork to do – which he despised. He also despised hunting, because he didn't like to kill animals. Because he was exceptionally strong for his age, his father hired him out as a "day laborer" – chopping trees, digging out stumps, digging wells, building fences. He also worked as a ferryman, and he helped out at a blacksmith's shop.

What experience left an enormous impression on him?

When he was nineteen, he and a friend had a great adventure. They piloted a flatboat down the Mississippi River for an Indiana merchant. This trip took them all the way to New Orleans, a city that was one of several ports of entry for the slave trade. It was on this trip that he first observed a slave market, a sight he never forgot.

THE ILLINOIS YEARS

When did Abraham Lincoln move to Illinois?

The Lincoln family moved to Macon County, Illinois, in 1830; Abraham was 21. The next year the family moved to Coles County, Illinois, and Abraham struck out on his own. He moved to New Salem, a few miles north of present-day Springfield.

How did he earn his living before he became a lawyer?

He worked as a store clerk and as a postmaster. He also taught himself surveying, later working as a surveyor.

Did Mr. Lincoln have any experience with the military?

He was a captain in the militia (citizen army) and spent three months in the Black Hawk War. He never saw any action.

Why do people call Mr. Lincoln a "self-made man"?

Mr. Lincoln didn't have much formal schooling. He learned on his own what he needed to know to be a storekeeper, a surveyor and a lawyer. When he was young, he read as much as possible and practiced both arithmetic and higher mathematics until he understood the concepts. He never stopped learning.

Where did he practice law?

Mr. Lincoln began practicing law in 1841 in Springfield, Illinois. Throughout the rest of his life he worked as a lawyer. He traveled all over the state of Illinois and got to know many of the people – this helped him in elections.

Did he have any girlfriends?

Mr. Lincoln had romantic relationships with Ann Rutledge and Mary Owen. Ann died of typhoid fever at age 22, and he was severely depressed after this happened.

Whom did he marry?

After a tumultuous relationship, Mr. Lincoln married Mary Todd in 1842. A Kentuckian, Mary was more well-educated than Abraham and came from a wealthy, slave-owning family, though she was personally against slavery. She didn't think her sister (with whom she lived) would approve of the marriage, so she didn't tell her about the wedding until the day it happened.

Did Mr. and Mrs. Lincoln have any children?

The Lincolns had four children: Robert, William (Willie), Edward (Eddie), and Thomas (Tad). Eddie died at age three; Willie died when he was 12 and the Lincolns were living in the White

House. Tad died at 18, six years after Mr. Lincoln's assassination. By 1871, when she was 53, Mary Todd Lincoln had suffered the deaths of her husband and three of her four children.

What political experience did he have?

Mr. Lincoln believed politics was an honorable and important profession. Politics inspired him to become a lawyer. He served four terms in the Illinois legislature, beginning in 1834 when he was twenty-five years old (before he earned his license to practice law). He became a leading member of the state's Whig party, which opposed slavery and supported continued economic development of the western states (the building of railroads, canals, etc.).

In 1847 he was elected to the U.S. House of Representatives, where he served only one term. He opposed slavery in new territories and spoke in favor of gradual emancipation of slaves. When his term was over, he returned to Illinois to concentrate on his law practice, but he often spoke out against slavery. He did not think it should be allowed to extend into the territories.

Why were the Lincoln-Douglas debates so important?

Mr. Douglas and Mr. Lincoln opposed each other in the election to the Illinois Senate in 1858. The debates made them both famous, and they were both chosen by their political parties to run for President.

THE WASHINGTON YEARS

What was Mr. Lincoln's public view of slavery?

Mr. Lincoln believed that slavery was a great evil and frequently said so. However, as a lawyer, and as someone for whom the printed word had always been important, he also believed that laws must be obeyed until they could be changed. Here are some common views of slavery during the 1850s and how Mr. Lincoln felt about each of them:

- Pro-slavery advocates justified slavery on political, economic and cultural grounds, even though they may have had moral misgivings. Mr. Lincoln agreed that the federal government could not interfere with slavery where it already existed. However, he thought that the government could, and should, outlaw slavery in any of the new territories the U.S. acquired.

- Self-liberationists were slaves escaped out of slave states into the free states, and often into Canada. Mr. Lincoln believed that, strictly under the current law, slaveholders had the right to lay claim to their runaway slaves.

- Gradual emancipationists believed that the slaves should be freed over a period of time and that slavery would eventually come to an end. Before the Civil War, Mr. Lincoln shared this belief.

- Abolitionists wanted to end slavery immediately. Before the war, Mr. Lincoln was not an abolitionist, because he knew that the task of finding jobs and homes and providing education for millions of enslaved peoples would be an almost impossible task.

When Mr. Lincoln signed the Emancipation Proclamation, freeing slaves in the Rebel states, he viewed this as a military action, similar to suspending the rights of citizens in wartime (in this case he was forcing economic hardship on Southern slaveholders).

What were some of the more unpopular decisions Lincoln made during the Civil War?

Mr. Lincoln suspended civil liberties during the Civil War. He allowed military arrests of civilians and allowed the military to keep suspects in jail for a long time awaiting trial. His decision to order a military draft was also very unpopular. In 1863, in New York, there were riots against the draft in which 300 people were killed.

What, besides the Civil War, occupied Mr. Lincoln's time as president?

During Mr. Lincoln's presidency, Congress passed The Morrill Act (the basis for today's state universities) and the Homestead Act (which encouraged settlement of the West by offering potential settlers up to 160 acres of free land). Several measures were adopted involving communications, including the establishment of the first free mail delivery service, the first coast-to-coast telegraph operation, and a system of national banks. The Pacific Railway Acts of 1862 and 1864 granted federal support for construction of a transcontinental railroad.

Why was the election of 1864 unusual?

Countries in the middle of civil wars don't usually hold elections, but Mr. Lincoln insisted, and he thought he would not win. No U.S. President since Andrew Jackson had been re-elected to a second term.

How was President Lincoln assassinated?

Mr. Lincoln was shot with a pistol at close range by John Wilkes Booth, an actor. Booth and his co-conspirators, all Southern sympathizers who hated Mr. Lincoln passionately, had been planning for months; they actually intended to murder Secretary of State Edwin Stanton and Vice-President Andrew Johnson that same night, but only Booth was successful. Mr. Lincoln was moved to a boardinghouse across the street from Ford's Theatre where he was shot. He died early the next morning, April 15, 1865. Federal soldiers caught up with Booth eleven days later; he was killed when he refused to surrender.

TIMELINE OF ABRAHAM LINCOLN'S LIFE
1809-1865

A child in Kentucky

1809   Abraham Lincoln is born in a one-room log cabin near present-day Hodgenville, Kentucky, on February 12. His parents are Thomas and Nancy Lincoln. His sister Sarah is two years older.

1811   The Lincoln family moves to a 230-acre farm on Knob Creek, ten miles from Abraham's birthplace.

1812   Abraham's brother Thomas is born. He dies as an infant.

1815   Young Abraham attends a log schoolhouse.

A youth in Indiana

1816   The Lincoln family crosses the Ohio River and settles in the backwoods of Indiana.

1817   Abraham shoots a wild turkey and decides never to go hunting again.

1818   Abraham's mother dies of "milk sickness."

1819   Abraham's father, Thomas, marries a widow, Sarah Bush Johnston.

1828   Sarah Lincoln Gregson, Abraham's sister, dies while giving birth. The same year, Abraham takes his first flatboat trip to New Orleans.

A man in Illinois

1830   Abraham moves with his father and stepmother to Illinois.

1831   Abraham takes his second flatboat trip to New Orleans. When he returns, he moves to New Salem, Illinois, on his own. In the next five years he works as a store clerk, a postmaster and a surveyor.

1832   Mr. Lincoln runs for the Illinois General Assembly but loses that election. He enlists in the militia and is elected captain of his company, serving a total of three months during the Black Hawk War.

1834   Mr. Lincoln is elected to the Illinois General Assembly (he serves four terms).

1837   Mr. Lincoln moves to Springfield, Illinois, and starts to practice law.

1842   He marries Mary Todd, a Kentuckian. They make their home in Illinois.

A public servant in Illinois and Washington, D.C.

1843   Mr. Lincoln runs for U.S. House of Representatives but loses the election.
The Lincolns' first son, Robert, is born.

1846   Their second son, Edward (Eddy), is born.
Mr. Lincoln is elected to the U.S. House of Representatives; serves two years.

1847   The Lincoln family moves to Washington, D.C.

1850   Eddy Lincoln dies.
William (Willy) Lincoln is born.

1853   Lincoln's fourth son, Thomas (Tad), is born.

1855   Mr. Lincoln runs for U.S. Senate but loses.

1856   He helps organize the new anti-slavery Republican party of Illinois.

1858   Mr. Lincoln runs again for U.S. Senate. His debates with opponent Stephen Douglas attract national attention, but he loses that election.

1860   Mr. Lincoln is nominated for the presidency in May. In a four-way race, he is elected President in November.

1861   Abraham Lincoln is inaugurated as President of the United States of America on March 4. The U.S. Civil War begins on April 12.

1862   Willie Lincoln, age 11, dies.

1863   On January 1, Mr. Lincoln signs the Emancipation Proclamation, legally freeing slaves in Rebel states. He delivers the Gettysburg Address on November 19.

1864   Mr. Lincoln is re-elected and begins to serve a second term as President.

1865   On March 4, he delivers his Second Inaugural Address. Abraham Lincoln is assassinated on April 14 at Ford's Theater in Washington, D.C., by John Wilkes Booth. He dies early the next morning.

TIMELINE OF EVENTS DURING MR. LINCOLN'S LIFE

1809   James Madison is inaugurated President of the U.S. Abraham Lincoln is born.

1812   In the War of 1812, the United States goes to war against the United Kingdom.

1815   The Battle of New Orleans is fought after the peace treaty ending the War of 1812.

1816   Indiana, the 19th state, is admitted to the Union as a free state.

1817   James Monroe is inaugurated President of the U.S.

1818   Congress limits the number of stars on the American flag to 13, for the original colonies. Illinois becomes the 21st state.

1819   The first steamship crosses the Atlantic Ocean.

1820   The Missouri Compromise brings Maine, a free state, and Missouri, a slave state, into the Union. The Union now consists of 12 free states and 12 slave states.

1825   The Erie Canal opens, connecting the Great Lakes with the Atlantic Ocean.

John Quincy Adams is inaugurated President of the U.S.

1827   John James Audubon publishes "Birds of America."

1829   Andrew Jackson is inaugurated President of the U.S.

1830   Indian Removal Act allows the federal government to force Native Americans to exchange their lands in the east for lands in the west.

1835   Texas gains freedom from Mexico in the War of Texas Independence which ends 1836.

1837   Martin Van Buren is inaugurated President of the U.S.

1838   Removal of Cherokee Indians to Oklahoma (from Georgia) on the Trail of Tears results in thousands of deaths.

People against slavery organize the Underground Railroad, a network of people who help slaves escape to the North and even into Canada where slavery is against the law.

1839   Abner Doubleday lays out the first baseball field in Cooperstown, New York, and conducts the first baseball game ever played.

1841   First governor of the Indiana Territory, William Henry Harrison is inaugurated President of the U.S. He dies one month after taking the oath of office, and Vice-President John Tyler becomes President.

1842　Boston and Albany are connected by the first American railroad.

1844　The first telegraph message is sent by inventor Samuel Morse.

1845　James K. Polk is inaugurated President of the U.S.

1846　War with Mexico begins. In 1848, the U.S. defeats Mexico and gains much of the territory now known as the American Southwest.

1848　The first women's rights convention takes place in Seneca Falls, New York.

　　　　Discovery of gold at Sutter's Fort leads to the California Gold Rush. Thousands of prospectors pour into California seeking their fortunes.

　　　　Harriet Tubman escapes to the North and begins serving in the Underground Railroad.

1849　Kentuckian Zachary Taylor, hero of the Mexican War, is inaugurated President of the U.S. He dies in 1850 and Millard Fillmore becomes President.

　　　　Amelia Bloomer designs and wears the first pants for women.

1850　The Compromise of 1850 admits California as a free state, allows people in the New Mexico and Utah territories to decide for themselves about slavery, and prohibits slave markets in the District of Columbia.

1852　*Uncle Tom's Cabin*, a novel written by Harriet Beecher Stowe about the cruelties of slavery, is published and sells over one million copies in one year. The novel helps change attitudes towards African-Americans and slavery.

1853　Franklin Pierce is inaugurated President of the U.S.

1854　Opponents of slavery set up the Republican party, which advocates modernizing the United States by investing in higher education, banking, industry and railroads. It will rise to power in the presidential election of 1860 with Abraham Lincoln as its nominee.

1855　Former slave Frederick Douglass publishes his autobiography, *My Bondage and My Freedom.*

1857　James Buchanan is inaugurated President of the U.S.

　　　　After being brought to free territory by his owner, a slave named Dred Scott sues for his freedom, but the court rules that he had never ceased to be a slave, denies that he was a citizen, and denies him the right to sue.

1859　John Brown leads an armed raid on the federal arsenal at Harper's Ferry, Virginia; he is caught and executed.

　　　　The nation's first oil well is drilled in Oklahoma.

1860　In November, Abraham Lincoln wins election at the end of his presidential campaign.

1861 Abraham Lincoln is inaugurated President of the U.S.

Confederates open fire on Fort Sumter, South Carolina, beginning the Civil War.

South Carolina, Georgia, Alabama, Mississippi, Florida and Louisiana withdraw from the United States and form the Confederate States of America.

1862 Union forces capture Ford Henry, Fort Donelson, Jacksonville, and New Orleans; they are defeated at second Battle of Bull Run and Fredericksburg.

1863 During Lincoln's first term, West Virginia secedes from Virginia and joins the Union as a free state.

Confederate victories occur at Chancellorsville and Chickamauga; Union victories occur at Gettysburg, Vicksburg and Chattanooga.

Roller skating is introduced to the United States.

1864 During Lincoln's first term, Nevada becomes the 36th state.

Union General Sherman takes Atlanta, marches through Georgia.

1865 Lincoln is inaugurated for a second term as President on March 4.

Confederate general Robert E. Lee surrenders to Union general Ulysses S. Grant at Appomattox Courthouse, Virginia, on April 9.

Lincoln is shot at Ford's Theater, Washington, D.C., on April 14. He dies April 15.

The 13th Amendment to the Constitution of the United States is ratified in December, abolishing slavery everywhere in the U.S.

A LINCOLN VOCABULARY

To understand Abraham Lincoln and his legacy, students should know the meaning of the following words:

In the 1800s (19th Century), an **abolitionist** was a person who wanted to end slavery immediately. To **abolish** something means to get rid of it.

An **amendment** is a change made in a legal document.

An **assassin** is a person who kills an important person, such as a President.

An **armory** is where the military keeps its guns.

The **Cabinet** includes the President's closest advisors appointed to positions of Secretary.

The **border states** (Kentucky, Maryland, Missouri and Delaware) permitted slavery but did not secede from the Union to join the Confederacy.

The **cavalry** consists of soldiers on horseback.

A **campaign** includes the speeches, visits and other work done to win an election.

A **casualty** is a soldier who can no longer fight because he is dead, wounded, captured as a prisoner, or is missing in action.

A **civil war** is a war fought between groups of people of the same nation. The U.S. Civil War lasted from 1861 to 1865.

The **Compromise of 1850** was a collection of several U.S. laws that attempted to balance the interests of slave-holding and non-slavery states. This bi-partisan measure delayed the Civil War.

The **Confederacy**, or Confederate States of America, was the name the states that seceded from the Union gave themselves. The Confederacy lasted from 1861 to 1865. Kentuckian Jefferson Davis was its only President.

A **constitution** is a set of laws that define a government, outlining what it can and cannot do.

A **document** is written or printed information.

The **Emancipation Proclamation** was President Lincoln's formal announcement that freed slaves in the Confederate states.

To **enlist** is to sign up for military service.

Federal refers to the federal government (that is, the United States government).

A **fugitive** is a person who has run away from facing consequences for breaking the law.

The **Fugitive Slave Law** was passed by Congress in 1850. It was meant to tighten enforcement of returning runaway slaves, but it actually resulted in increasing the number of abolitionists.

An **inauguration** is the formal swearing-in ceremony during which the elected President begins a term in office.

The **infantry** consists of soldiers on foot.

An **orator** is a skilled public speaker.

A **plantation** is a very large crop farm, usually located in a warm climate. Plantations in the American South before the Civil War depended on slaves to do most of the work.

A **platform** is the list of views and programs supported by a candidate for office.

A **proclamation** is an announcement.

Rankings in the military are as follows: private, corporal, sergeant, lieutenant, captain, major, colonel, general. Sergeant and corporal are non-commissioned officers.

A **Rebel** was a Confederate soldier.

To **repeal** is to reverse a law or an official act of government.

To **secede** is to formally withdraw from a group or organization.

An action that is **unconstitutional** goes against a nation's constitution.

The **Union** is the United States of America. In the Civil War, it means the Northern states that remained loyal to the federal government and did not secede.

A **Yankee** was a soldier who fought for the Union Army in the Civil War in support of the Northern states that did not secede.

LINCOLN

Chapter Two

Ten Activities For Learning About Mr. Lincoln

Activity #1

CREATING A TIMELINE

All historical activities must begin with a timeline for context. If young people are to make sense of history, they must have a sense of what happened when – and how significant events are connected. With a basic timeline understood, students have scaffolding in place upon which to attach new information. When they no longer have to deal with an isolated list of facts, history reveals its own logic – and then its magic begins to work.

In this activity students research events that would have made headlines during Mr. Lincoln's time and then create an illustrated timeline to be displayed on classroom walls.

PROCEDURE

Materials: colored pencils or markers, large index cards or 8 1/2 x 11 sheets of white paper, list of significant events from 1809-1865

Introducing the activity

Tell the students that the world changes rapidly. Together, brainstorm changes that have occurred since they were born (e.g., text messaging, the war in Iraq, hybrid cars, the iPhone, election of the first African-American President).

What was the world like in Lincoln's time? It changed significantly during the 56 years he was alive. When Lincoln was born there were 17 states in the Union; at the time of his death, there were 36. There were two major wars in Lincoln's lifetime. When he was born, most people cooked in fireplaces, whether they lived on the Kentucky frontier or a New York City mansion; by 1865, most homes outside of the frontier had stoves and kitchens. Railroads, baseball, steamships, the telegraph – all these were unknown in 1809.

Doing the research

Separate each date/event on the "Timeline of Events During Mr. Lincoln's Life" handout (page 22) by photocopying the page and cutting it into strips. For each date/event, students are to conduct whatever research is necessary so that they can draw a picture representing the particular event on an index card or piece of copy paper. Tell them to be sure to put the date in the upper right hand corner of the card in large letters. (Create an example to show them.) They should also write a few words announcing the event at the bottom of the card. Have books about Lincoln and the 19th Century available so students can look for examples.

This can be a homework or classroom assignment. If you choose to do it in class, distribute topics so as to accommodate different student interests and abilities. (Some items require less research than others.) This is to balance the fact that even though you encourage students to be careful and accurate, one student will create five cards in the time it takes another to complete just one.

Establishing the timeline

As students are ready to create their own cards, show them the two cards you have already prepared: one depicts Abraham Lincoln's birth in 1809 and the other depicts his death by assassination in 1865. Choose a space on the classroom wall for the timeline: the best timelines wrap around the wall, perhaps starting at one side of the door and continuing around the room to end at the other side of the door. With tape, fix a piece of yarn, a strip of paper of some sort, or blue painter's tape to physically create the timeline, putting it at the students' average eye level. Tape the card depicting Lincoln's birth at one end and the card depicting his death at the other. As students complete their cards, put each in its proper place on the timeline. As the cards mount up, you may need to adjust their placement.

When all the cards are up, have the students come up with some categories to group some of the cards together. You might want to use this sequence: Abraham Lincoln in Kentucky; Abraham Lincoln in Indiana; Abraham Lincoln in Illinois; Abraham Lincoln in Washington, D.C. Students may have other ideas for organizing the research.

Follow-up

The timeline should stay on the wall throughout the students' study of Lincoln; both you and the students should refer to it so that whatever they learn about Mr. Lincoln or about the 19th Century is anchored in time. New cards can be added as the occasion arises.

FURTHER EXPLORATION

Another good timeline activity is for each student to create his/her very own timeline book. You can have students purchase a blank book or create one by folding sheets of paper together and stapling or sewing them at the center fold. (Use 14 pieces of white legal-sized copy paper to make a 56-page book, one page for each of Mr. Lincoln's 56 years. Add one more sheet to create front and back covers.) Students can draw or paste illustrations on the appropriate pages as they learn more about Mr. Lincoln.

One more possibility is for students to create a chronological PowerPoint presentation.

RESOURCES

Abraham Lincoln Bicentennial 2009 – www.lincolnbicentennial.gov
> The interactive timeline at this site will capture students' attention quickly.

The History Place – www.historyplace.com/lincoln
> This site contains a far more detailed timeline of Mr. Lincoln's life, with speeches and photographs embedded. There is a link to another timeline for the Civil War.

Abraham Lincoln Presidential Library and Museum – www.alplm.org/timeline/timeline.html
> This excellent and very well-designed timeline will take students through Mr. Lincoln's life year by year.

Activity #2

CREATING PICTURE BOOKS

Toward the end of your study of Mr. Lincoln, after students are somewhat familiar with his life, his humor, his compassion, and his determination, have them create picture books for younger children. This is an excellent activity if you've been reading Carl Sandburg's *Abe Lincoln Grows Up* aloud to your students.

PROCEDURE

Introducing the activity

Read your students two or three of the many excellent picture books about Lincoln (some recent ones are listed on the next two pages). Many of the picture books that are written these days aren't just for the very young. Some are written with words that make more sense to older students, and the illustrations provide insights not found in the text. They are very worthy of study. As you read, ask students questions not only about the story, but about the illustrations as well. Why has the artist chosen to depict this particular scene? What do they learn about 19th Century life from the illustrations?

Conducting the activity

Invite the students to create their own picture book about some aspect of Mr. Lincoln's life. (It works best if you have some examples to show them. The first time you do this, you'll need to create one on your own.) Following are some ideas for topics, but give the students the option of choosing or creating their own. Refer them to Carl Sandburg's *Abe Lincoln Grows Up* or other books about Lincoln's early life.

• When he was very young, Abraham was rescued by his good friend Austin after he fell into Knob Creek. Austin held out a long pole, and when Abraham was able to catch hold of it, Austin pulled him to the bank. *What happens when the two boys returned home, their clothes dripping wet?*

• When Abraham Lincoln was a teenager, his stepmother often joked that he was so tall he would leave footprints on her ceiling. When she was away from the house, Abraham persuaded a young cousin to dip his bare feet in the mud. Then he took the boy inside, held him upside-down and had him "walk" across the ceiling. *What does his stepmother do when she finds the footprints on the ceiling?*

• President Lincoln's young sons, Tad and Willie, were permitted the run of the White House. They also brought their many pets inside. *What happens when Tad's pet goat interrupts a meeting between President Lincoln and his advisors in the oval office?*

Each book should be at least eight pages. Instruct students to keep their stories brief: Each page should have two or three sentences at most. They may draw pictures or paste in illustrations found on the Internet. Make an eight-page book by folding two legal-sized sheets of copy paper in half; assemble and number the pages. Create a wrap-around cover on a third sheet of legal-sized paper; laminate it. Then wrap the cover around the assembled inside pages, and staple or sew all the pieces together in the middle fold (spine).

Concluding the activity

If you can partner with a younger classroom, you might be able to arrange a trip so that the student authors can read their own books to the younger children.

RESOURCES

Here are some excellent recently-published picture books about Mr. Lincoln:

Borden, Louise W. *A. Lincoln and Me.* Illustrated by Ted Lewin. Scholastic, 2001.

> A sensitive teacher tells a boy "skinny as a beanpole and tall for my age" how much he has in common with Mr. Lincoln. He comes to believe that if Lincoln could go on to greatness, anyone can.

Brenner, Margaret. *Abe Lincoln's Hat.* Illustrated by Donald Cook. Random House, 1994.

> Lots of humorous anecdotes enliven this picture-book introduction to Abraham Lincoln.

Krensky, Stephen. *Abe Lincoln and the Muddy Pig.* Illustrated by Gersom Griffith. Aladdin, 2002.

> The author uses the story of how Abe Lincoln once rescued a drowning pig – even though he was wearing his best suit and was on his way to make an important speech – to reveal much about his character.

Polacco, Patricia. *Pink and Say.* Philomel, 1994.

> This picture book about an interracial friendship between two 15-year-old Union soldiers during the Civil War is honest, heart wrenching, and beautifully told. The fact that the white soldier once shook Abraham Lincoln's hand is a central image for the story. "Let me touch the hand that touched Mr. Lincoln," the African-American boy says to his friend, and as the novel ends, the survivor tells his children, who tell theirs, that they have touched the hand that touched the hand.... (Intended for intermediate students, but meaningful to any age.)

St. George, Judith. *Stand Tall, Abe Lincoln.* Illustrated by Matt Faulkner. Philomel, 2008.

> This picture book is more comprehensive than most. It is an excellent account of the years Abraham Lincoln spent living in poverty on the Kentucky and Indiana frontiers and emphasizes the influence of his stepmother on his will to succeed in life and work.

Turner, Ann. *Abe Lincoln Remembers*. Illustrated by Wendell Minor. HarperCollins, 2001.

   The language in this picture book is written in first person, as if Lincoln is looking back on his own life and recalling what was most important. Written for young people, but older ones will enjoy the musical language and beautiful illustrations as well.

Winnick, Karen, B. *Mr. Lincoln's Whiskers*. Boyds Mills, 1996.

   This book tells the story of an 11-year-old girl who wrote to Mr. Lincoln and encouraged him to grow a beard to get more votes. On the way to his inaugural, Mr. Lincoln met her and thanked her for her advice.

Van Steenwyk, Elizabeth. *When Abraham Talked to the Trees*. Illustrated by Bill Farnsworth. Eerdmans, 2000.

   Focusing on Lincoln's youth, this picture-book biography traces the growth of his love for words and reading despite an impoverished childhood and lack of formal education.

Winters, Kay. *Abe Lincoln: The Boy Who Loved Books.* Illustrated by Nancy Carpenter. Simon & Schuster, 2003.

   The free verse narrative in this biography emphasizes Lincoln's childhood and adolescence. Pages are dominated by illustrations that include many details of pioneer life. A good choice for reading aloud.

Activity #3

HISTORICAL IDENTITIES: THE 1830 CENSUS

Students learn more and care more about history when they can connect emotionally with it. An excellent way to connect students emotionally with history is to give them opportunities to live imaginatively in the past. Once they have a foothold in past time, they will relate other historic information to this experience, establishing that all-important sequence.

In this activity, students build a society only with information that appears on a particular year's census rolls. The process is especially useful for growth of their understanding of economic and government systems.

If possible, schedule this activity after you've taken a trip to the Lincoln Boyhood National Memorial or The Abraham Lincoln Birthplace National Historic Site.

PROCEDURE

Introducing the activity

Tell the students that in 1830, when Abraham Lincoln was 21, the Lincoln family moved to a new home near Decatur, Illinois. Drawing from their knowledge of pioneer life, what do they think the town was like? What did the stores sell? What kind of people lived there? What did they do for a living?

Tell students that the U.S. Constitution requires that a census be taken every ten years (2000, 2010, etc.). 1830 was a census year. In 1830, the U.S. census listed the person's name, age, gender, color, and territory or country of birth. Census details also indicated whether the person attended school or was married within the year, whether the person could read or write if over age of twenty, whether the person was deaf-mute, blind or insane, whether the person was a fugitive from any state, the value of any real estate the person owned, and the occupation of any male over the age of 15.

Conducting the activity

Students will imagine that they live in the year 1830 in a new settlement on the American frontier. The teacher will play the part of the census-taker who questions students one by one; but it's an open forum, and others may have comments or suggestions regarding what kinds of information should be sought. Have fun with this. Students are free to use their own names or invent new ones for themselves. They must invent their own occupations, choosing work that existed in 1830, and they may choose to be any age. Invariably, this activity takes on a kind of synergy, and a community emerges, fully populated with all kinds (and ages) of individuals, an economic system, a local government, institutions and more.

The activity demands a high degree of teacher participation and requires that the teacher be especially knowledgeable about the era under consideration. It is the teacher, in the role of census-taker, who focuses students' imaginations to keep everything historically accurate. No anachronisms are allowed in this game. (Their historic roles are particularly difficult for girls to accept.) The census-taker cannot tell students who they are, but he/she can guide them or make suggestions. For example, if the year under consideration is 1830, the teacher can point out that the names "L'keshia" or "Jaylon" or "Brittney" were not common in the U.S., and so those students would have to create new names for themselves; students named "Millie" or "Daniel," on the other hand, could keep their own names if they like. This small, first correction of anachronisms opens students' minds to the enormity of the differences to come. As the questions progress, family associations and origins emerge, giving the instructor opportunities to talk about typical westward migration. Occupations give the census-taker an opportunity to make suggestions (e.g., with a river running through it, your town might benefit from a sawmill), corrections (there was no electric power in 1830; trees are sawn by hand), and elaborations (your closest market is Louisville; how are you going to get the timber there?) – but the decisions belong to the students.

A variation that would make the game playable with larger groups of students is to assign the students their identities, in the form of completed census reports, rather than letting them choose their own. Given some historical parameters, students can work in groups to form a community by answering a series of questions on their own. This could be set up as a board game, with a set of steps leading to a particular goal (self-sufficiency?) or time period ("Congratulations, you've survived the 1830s!") "Catastrophe cards" could be a part of the game, giving each group of students a certain obstacle a family or their whole community has to overcome to reach the goal.

Concluding the activity

This activity has great potential for Language Arts follow-up in the classroom. Students are generally very motivated to write about their first-hand experiences "living" in history, especially in journal or letter format.

RESOURCES

For some basic information about frontier communities, read *If You Grew Up With Abraham Lincoln*, by Ann McGovern.

Census data is available online at the Historical Census Browser, University of Virginia Library, http://fisher.lib.virginia.edu/collections/stats/histcensus.

Activity #4

SING THE SONGS LINCOLN KNEW

To understand the 19th Century, students should listen to music popular of the time and analyze lyrics to discover more about culture and politics of that era.

PROCEDURE

Introducing the lesson

Tell students that long before there was recorded music, before radio, television, movies or the Internet, people across the nation still knew and sang the same songs. Some songs were written by composers and were distributed through magazines or as sheet music. Other songs – called folk songs – might be hundreds of years old; no one knows for sure because they were passed along from one generation to the next.

The first American songs were tied to the musical traditions of the British Isles. Hymns, game songs, ballads, dance songs, humorous songs, and drinking songs were often based on British models. Immigrants from other European countries contributed to American songs, and the African-Americans brought to America as slaves added music and rhythms of their native lands.

Early in the 19th Century, Americans began writing their own American music, rather than putting new words to old songs. The first songs were written for minstrel shows and quickly spread across the country. People learned the new music from inexpensive sheet music; the songs were also printed in various magazines.

Conducting the lesson

Song lyrics are provided with this lesson, along with some background for each song. Play the melodies for students, giving a brief introduction as you do so. (You can find recordings online through iTunes and other websites.) Then divide students into groups, giving each group one of the songs to analyze. Give them 15 minutes to do so, and then ask each group to report their findings to the class.

Depending on the maturity of your class, you might mention the following:

- The singing of the song "Dixie," by far the most popular song of the mid-19th Century, is sometimes considered offensive because it is connected with the ideology of the slaveholding South. During the Civil War, the song was adopted as the unofficial anthem of the Confederacy. Its lyrics tell of a person longing for his home in the South.

- Words change meaning over time. For example, the word "gay," up through the 1950s or 1960s, meant "happy." It appears in many 19th Century songs; Stephen Foster, the best-known American songwriter of the 19th Century, often used it for its easy rhyme (play, say, away, day). Another language shift was apparent when, in 1928, the Kentucky Legislature adopted Foster's "My Old Kentucky Home" as the state song but changed Foster's original lyrics from "darkies" to "people."

Concluding the lesson

Sing the songs as often as you like – they're American standards that students ought to know.

FURTHER EXPLORATION

Challenge students to develop a modern playlist of songs that relate to Lincoln's life and the challenges he faced, both as he grew up and during his years in the White House.

Challenge students to find the lyrics of a song that deals with how we live in the 21st Century.

RESOURCES

Recordings

Folk musician Jerry Ernst performs songs from the mid-19th Century on period instruments, including a small parlor organ and a fretless banjo. His music is available through the CD Baby website (http://cdbaby.com/group/jerund). Several of his CDs of mid 19th Century popular songs are also available on iTunes.

> *The Adventures of Billy Barlow*
> *Angel Band*
> *The Road to Richmond*
> *In Love and War*
> *Night March to Gettysburg*

On his CD *Abe Lincoln In Song (2007)*, Chris Vallilo combines storytelling, contemporary music, and period folk songs to bring Mr. Lincoln and his times to life. Vallillo also performs the program for schools and community organizations. Check his website (www.ginridge.com) for more information. The CD is available on iTunes.

Several recordings of music from the Civil War era are available on iTunes. *Songs of the Civil War* (1991) is particularly good; artists include Kate & Anna McGarrigle, Rufus Wainwright, Kathy Mattea, John Hartford, Sweet Honey in the Rock, and Judy Collins. The collection includes "Give Us a Flag," by Richie Havens, which deals with African-American soldiers in the Union army; it refers to Mr. Lincoln, Company A (the first unit of former slaves), and the Massachusetts 54th (the regiment featured in the movie *Glory*).

Websites

Hundreds of full versions of songs popular in the 19th Century are available through the Abraham Lincoln Historical Digitation Project. The files are organized by the songbooks in which they appeared – the same song books that might have been handed out while Mr. Lincoln campaigned for President. Find them at http://lincoln.lib.niu.edu/sound.html.

Text and midi files of many historic songs are available on a website of "public domain" music, http://pdmusic.org. The site is useful for providing song melodies – no lyrics are sung in these recordings, but they provide sufficient background for a simple singalong.

Sheet Music

Find sheet music for any of these songs online through Google Image or Wikipedia. All songs used in this lesson are in the public domain, so they can be copied and distributed to students royalty-free. You can also search for sheet music on the American Memory website, http://memory.loc.gov/ammem/scsmhtml/scsmhome.html.

MORE ON 19th CENTURY SONGS

There's no way of knowing if Mr. Lincoln actually knew the following songs, but they were widely known and sung during his lifetime.

1810s
The Star Spangled Banner, Blow the Man Down, The Girl I Left Behind Me, Yankee Doodle, Auld Lang Syne

1820s
On Top of Old Smoky, Hunters of Kentucky, Turkey in the Straw, The Old Oaken Bucket, Home Sweet Home

1830s
Rock of Ages, My Country 'Tis of Thee, Woodman Spare That Tree

1840s
Green Grow the Lilacs, Buffalo Gals, The Old Grey Goose, Jimmy Crack Corn, Oh Susanna, Camptown Races, Old Dan Tucker, Long Long Ago, 'Tis a Gift to Be Simple

1850s
Old Folks at Home, My Old Kentucky Home, Nellie Gray, Listen to the Mockingbird, The Yellow Rose of Texas

SONGS & LYRICS

OLD DOG TRAY (1853)

The morn of life is past,
And evening comes at last;
It brings me a dream of a once happy day,
Of merry forms I've seen
Upon the village green,
Sporting with my old dog Tray.

Chorus: Old dog Tray's ever faithful,
     Grief cannot drive him away,
     He's gentle, he is kind;
     I'll never, never find
     A better friend than old dog Tray.

The forms I call'd my own
Have vanished one by one,
The lov'd ones, the dear ones have all passed away;
Their happy smiles have flown,
Their gentle voices gone;
I've nothing left but old dog Tray.

Chorus

When thoughts recall the past
His eyes are on me cast;
I know that he feels what my breaking heart would say:
Although he cannot speak
I'll vainly, vainly seek
A better friend than old dog Tray.

Chorus

About the song ...

"Old Dog Tray" was written by Stephen Foster in 1853. The typical American song style in the mid-19th Century was a sentimental ballad, expressing the virtues of fidelity, honor, love, etc. These songs were usually about mothers, elders or marriageable young girls; however, addressing a much-loved pet was not unusual.

Stephen Foster, often called America's first professional songwriter, is regarded as one of the most successful composers of popular music that any American has ever produced. Some of his songs were used as minstrel show tunes, performed in "blackface" (white actors who painted their faces with burnt cork and pretended to be African-American). Although his songs are seen by some today as racist, Mr. Foster deplored racism, sympathized with the abolitionists, and tried to convince white performers to portray black people with dignity. "Old Dog Tray" is the first of Foster's songs in which race is not identifiable.

Analyzing the lyrics ...

Have students figure out the meaning of the words "forms," "sporting," "cast," and "vainly" from the context. What does "upon the village green" mean? Tell students that styles of songs – just like clothes and cars and video games – change over time. Sentimentality in music is currently out of fashion, for the most part. Can students think of a song today that might be called "sentimental?" (Consider holiday songs.) Many songs popular in the 1850s dealt with death; do students know why?

LISTEN TO THE MOCKINGBIRD (1855)

I'm dreaming now of Hally, sweet Hally, sweet Hally
I'm dreaming now of Hally
For the thought of her is one that never dies
She's sleeping in the valley, the valley, the valley
She's sleeping in the valley
And the mockingbird is singing where she lies.

Chorus: Listen to the mockingbird
              Listen to the mockingbird
              The mockingbird still singing o'er her grave
              Listen to the mockingbird
              Listen to the mockingbird
              Still singing where the weeping willows wave.

Ah! well I yet remember, remember, remember
Ah! well I yet remember,
When we gather'd in the cotton side by side
'Twas in the mild September, September, September
Twas in the mild September,
And the mockingbird was singing far and wide.

Chorus

When the charms of spring awaken, awaken, awaken,
When the charms of spring awaken,
And the mockingbird is singing on the bough.
I feel like one forsaken, forsaken, forsaken.
I feel like one forsaken,
Since my Hally is no longer with me now.

Chorus

About the song ...

The lyrics of "Listen to the Mockingbird" were written by Septimus Winner under the pseudonym "Alice Hawthorne." Mr. Winner had a music publishing business, and he took the tune he used for "Mockingbird" from an African-American employee, paying him $5 for the rights. The song became extremely popular; by the turn of the century, several million copies of the sheet music had been sold. Several sources remark that it was Mr. Lincoln's favorite song.

Analyze the lyrics ...

What do students think might account for the popularity of this song? (Despite being about death, it has a very upbeat melody. Also, the repetition makes it easy to remember.) Like "Old Dog Tray," it deals with death. Why was death such a popular theme in the 1850s (this was before the Civil War)? Ask students why Mr. Lincoln might have liked this song so much. Had death touched his life? (Yes, his mother, sister, and infant brother all died when he was young. His four-year-old son, Eddy, died in 1850, and his twelve-year-old son, Willie, died while Mr. Lincoln was President.)

NELLIE GRAY (1856)

In a long green, valley on the old Kentucky shore
Sure I've whiled many happy hours away,
Just a sitting and a singing by the little cabin door
Where lived my darling Nellie Gray

When the moon had climbed the mountain, and stars were shining bright
I'd take my darling Nellie Gray
And we'd float down the river in my little red canoe
While my banjo so sweetly I would play

One night I went to see her, but she's gone the neighbors say
And the white man had bound her with his chain
They have taken her to Georgia for to wear her life away
As she toils in the cotton and the cane

Oh, my darling Nellie Gray, they have taken you away
I'll never see my darling anymore
They have taken you to Georgia for to work your life away
And you're gone from that old Kentucky shore.

Now my canoe is under water, and my banjo is unstrung
I am tired of living, anymore
My eyes shall be cast downward, and my songs will be unsung
While I stay on the old Kentucky shore

Now my eyes are getting dimmer and I cannot see the light
Hark there's someone a-knocking at my door
Oh I hear the angels coming and I see my Nellie Gray
So farewell to the old Kentucky shore

Oh my darling Nellie Gray, up in heaven, so they say
And they'll never take you from me, anymore
Oh I'm coming, coming, coming, as the angels clear the way
So farewell to the old Kentucky shore

About the song ...

"Darling Nellie Gray" was composed by Benjamin Hanby, a college student, in 1856 as a fundraiser for a Kentucky slave who had escaped to the North by crossing the Ohio River. Henby's father, William, worked with the Underground Railroad and was trying to purchase the young man's wife. It quickly caught the attention of the public and became very popular in the North. Even though its composer is known, the song has passed into the folk tradition. Many different versions exist.

Analyze the lyrics ...

Who is singing the song? What details of his life can you find in the lyrics? Tell students that songs like this were written to rally the public against slavery. What view does the lyricist have on slavery? How can you tell? What clues does the song provide about the kind of life Nellie can expect to have in Georgia? Why would this be different from her life in Kentucky? What do the ruined canoe and the silent banjo symbolize in the fifth verse?

LINCOLN AND LIBERTY TOO (1860)

Hurrah for the choice of the nation
Our chieftain so brave and so true
We'll go for the great reformation
For Lincoln and Liberty too!

Chorus: We'll go for the son of Kentucky
The hero of Hoosierdom through
The pride of the "Suckers" so lucky
For Lincoln and Liberty too!

They'll find what by felling and mauling
Our railmaker statesman can do
For the people are everywhere calling
For Lincoln and Liberty too

Chorus

Then up with the banner so glorious
The star-spangled red, white, and blue
We'll fight till our banner's victorious
For Lincoln and Liberty too.

Chorus

Our David's good sling is unerring
The Slavocrat's giant he slew
Then shout for the freedom preferring
For Lincoln and Liberty too.

Chorus

About the song ...

"Lincoln and Liberty Too" is a patriotic song written for Mr. Lincoln's 1860 presidential campaign. Every American President since George Washington has used a campaign theme song to inspire supporters. Franklin D. Roosevelt chose the cheery "Happy Days Are Here Again" to give people hope in the midst of the Great Depression. Bill Clinton chose the Fleetwood Mac song "Don't Stop Thinking About Tomorrow" to inspire progressive thinking toward the future.

Ask students to think about the differences between modern-day presidential campaigns and 19th Century campaigns. Before radio, television and the Internet, candidates made their way slowly across the nation (which consisted of 33 states in 1860) to meet face-to-face with voters. The singing of campaign songs was part of every march, every parade, every public event. Songbooks containing lyrics and information about the candidates' platforms were handed out. New lyrics were often attached to familiar melodies to make the songs easier to sing. The melody for "Lincoln and Liberty Too" has actually been used for many songs but is probably best known as "Rosin the Beau."

Analyze the lyrics ...

Ask students what they learn about Lincoln's life from this song's lyrics. By profession, Mr. Lincoln was a lawyer: why didn't the lyricist include that information? What do the lines "Our David's good sling is unerring" and "The Slavocrat's giant he slew" mean? Do students think that people decided to vote for Mr. Lincoln because of the song?

To which three states does the lyricist connect Mr. Lincoln? Ask students to look at the third line of the chorus. Tell them that the word "sucker" in the third line doesn't refer to a gullible person (as in "there's one born every minute") but to residents of Illinois, where the creeks and lakes were full of suckerfish.

Tell or remind the students about various propaganda devices (repetition, appeal to emotions, bandwagon approach). What elements of this song are still found in political campaigns? Do students know the songs connected with recent presidential campaigns?

THE BATTLE HYMM OF THE REPUBLIC (1861)

Mine eyes have seen the glory of the coming of the Lord.
He is trampling out the vintage where the grapes of wrath are stored;
He hath loosed the fateful lightning of His terrible swift sword:
His truth is marching on.

Glory, glory, hallelujah! Glory, glory, hallelujah! Glory, glory, hallelujah!
His truth is marching on.

I have seen Him in the watch-fires of a hundred circling camps,
They have builded Him an altar in the evening dews and damps;
I can read His righteous sentence by the dim and flaring lamps:
His day is marching on.

Glory, glory, hallelujah! Glory, glory, hallelujah! Glory, glory, hallelujah!
His day is marching on.

I have read a fiery gospel writ in burnished rows of steel:
"As ye deal with my contemners, so with you my grace shall deal;
Let the Hero, born of woman, crush the serpent with His heel,
Since God is marching on."

Glory, glory, hallelujah! Glory, glory, hallelujah! Glory, glory, hallelujah!
Since God is marching on.

He has sounded forth the trumpet that shall never call retreat;
He is sifting out the hearts of men before His judgment-seat:
Oh, be swift, my soul, to answer Him! Be jubilant, my feet!
Our God is marching on.

Glory, glory, hallelujah! Glory, glory, hallelujah! Glory, glory, hallelujah!
Our God is marching on.

In the beauty of the lilies Christ was born across the sea,
With a glory in His bosom that transfigures you and me:
As He died to make men holy, let us die to make men free,
While God is marching on.

Glory, glory, hallelujah! Glory, glory, hallelujah! Glory, glory, hallelujah!
While God is marching on.

About the song ...

"The Battle Hymn of the Republic" was written by Julia Ward Howe, a writer and social activitist. As were many songs in that day, the lyrics were sung to a familiar tune, in this case, a Union marching song. Ms. Howe first heard it as "John Brown's Body." She liked the tune but not the coarse lyrics, which began with "John Brown's body lies a'mouldering in his grave," and wanted the troops to sing more uplifting words. The song was published on the front page of a popular magazine in 1861, and by 1862, had been reprinted in newspapers, in Army hymnbooks, in pamphlets, and as sheet music in all the major cities of the North. It remained popular through two centuries. Its lyrics appear repeatedly in Martin Luther King's speeches and writings.

Analyze the lyrics ...

Where does the imagery come from in this song? Why does Ms. Howe use so many phrases from the Bible? Why does she talk about wine in the first stanza? (Wine is the color of blood.) In the second verse, where are the camps, and what "sentence" is there? In the third verse, who is the hero and what does the serpent represent? If students are familiar with the Crusades, make some comparisons. The third verse uses the word "contemners," which means someone who scorns or has contempt. What are these individuals contemptuous of?

ABRAHAM'S TEA PARTY (1864)

We're going down to Dixie, boys
Upon a little ride
Our knapsacks on behind us, boys
And sabers by our side
Our Abraham invited us
Three hundred thousand strong
To come to tea, and here we are
We're coming right along!

Chorus   Heave, ho, laddie!
               We'll sing to Abe our song:
               We're coming, father Abraham,
               We're coming right along

And when we're down in Dixie, boys
"Old Abe" with us will be
One little job he'd have us do
Before we take our tea
There is a thief called "Rebel Jeff"
Who steals from Uncle Sam,
We'll catch, and him we'll introduce
To father Abraham.

Chorus

We'll make a present to the crews,
Of Beauregard and Lee,
Some pepper, grape, and canisters
Of strong gunpowder tea!
And when we've swept the rattlesnakes
Into the gulf and sea
We're coming, father Abraham,
We're coming home to tea!

Chorus

About the song ...

"Abraham's Tea Party" was written in 1864 by J.H. McNaughton in support of the war. Mr. Lincoln's call for an additional 600,000 volunteers was not greeted with enthusiasm by everyone.

Analyze the lyrics ...

What does the song suggest about the people who signed up to fight in the Union army? Why are they so willing to fight? What opinion do they seem to have of "Uncle Abe"? Why would this be important to include in this particular song?

Activity #5

TABLEAUX VIVANTS: SCENES FROM LINCOLN'S LIFE

Creating tableaux vivants was a popular form of entertainment 150 years ago, before there were movies or television. The phrase is French, and it means "living illustrations" or "stage pictures." (*Tableaux* is plural, while *tableau* is singular.) The tableau vivant technique has been used to stage everything from religious presentations to burlesque entertainments. Performers in a presentation of tableau vivant *(pronounced tab-lo vee-vahn)* usually recreate a scene from a painting (e.g., DaVinci's "Last Supper"); they hold the pose while the audience views them. Occasionally, a narrator explains what is happening in the scene. Often, music is involved.

In this activity, students will recreate the scenes on the limestone panels that mark the entrance to the Lincoln Boyhood National Memorial in southern Indiana. Although you can teach this lesson by looking up the panels online, it works especially well after students take a field trip to the site. If you do this, have students look closely at the five limestone panels in the front of the Memorial Building. Point out individuals the artist has included in each panel, and ask students why they think these particular people are included. Take photos of each of the panels for later reference. (In case a field trip is not possible, panel images are provided in Chapter Five.)

PROCEDURE

Introducing the lesson

Show students the panels or photographs of the panels (found on 138 or online at http://showcase.netins.net/web/creative/lincoln/art/sculpt.htm). Tell them that artists make deliberate decisions about their works of art all the time, anticipating the effect that the completed piece will have on people who see it. Elmer Daniels, who sculpted the panels, was given the basic idea for the panels and a list of people, but he had to decide how to pose them and what else to include in each panel. Briefly identify each of the individuals on the panels. Ask students what else Mr. Daniels chose to include. Why, for example, would the artist choose to include a butter churn in the Kentucky panel and an axe in the Indiana panel?

Conducting the lesson

Divide the students into five groups and give each group one of the photos and a list of the individuals pictured on it. Tell the groups that their task is to recreate the image for the class. All students must play a role. If there are more people in the scene than there are group members, they may "borrow" someone from another group.

As they plan and rehearse their performances, each group will function differently. On the first day, let group members work through what they need on their own as much as you can. Step in only if they need a little guidance from you to divide up the work.

Encourage students to bring costume pieces and props from home. (You might want to have a few things on hand as well.) However, let them know that the costumes aren't really that important: their emphasis should be on holding the positions of each of the characters.

Each student is also responsible for researching the individual he or she is depicting. When students perform, they will all get into position (preferably behind a curtain). When the curtain is drawn, they will hold that position for about a minute. (Take a photo of them.) Then, one by one, the students will step out of the tableau, each announcing his or her name and saying or reading a few words about his/her relationship to Mr. Lincoln. Abraham Lincoln needs to be the last person remaining in each tableau; the curtain closes on him. (Students playing anonymous soldiers or laborers should feel free to make up some details about their lives.)

Give the groups two or three days to gather their materials, and set aside a day for practice. (It's a good idea to move to the gym or other open area so that all the groups can practice at the same time.) Hold the performance for another class or invite parents to watch.

Concluding the activity

Display photos of both the student groups and the panels. Have students respond to them (or to their tableau vivant experience) in writing.

RESOURCES

Here's a list of the individuals pictured in each of the panels:

KENTUCKY PANEL: 1809-1816. The Early Years

- Jesse Lafollette, the Lincoln family's neighbor at Knob Creek Farm
- Thomas Lincoln, Abraham's father
- Christopher Columbus Graham, doctor, scientist and frequent visitor at the Lincoln farm
- Abraham Lincoln, age 7
- Nancy Hanks Lincoln, Abraham's mother
- Sarah Lincoln, Abraham's sister, age 9
- Caleb Hazel, neighbor of the Lincolns and Abraham's second teacher

INDIANA PANEL: 1816-1830. The Boyhood Days of Lincoln

- James Gentry, wealthy farmer and merchant. Abraham frequently visited his home
- Josiah Crawford. Abraham worked for him three days to pay for a book he borrowed that was damaged by rain
- Aaron Grigsby, a neighbor who married Abraham's sister Sarah
- Abraham Lincoln, age about 19
- Dennis Hanks, Lincoln's cousin, who lived many years with the Lincoln family in Indiana
- Allen Gentry (son of James), friend of Abraham. The two went on a flatboat trip to New Orleans when Abraham was 19

ILLINOIS PANEL: 1830-1861. The Years of Political Ascendancy

Mr. Lincoln is congratulated on his election to the United States House of Representatives in 1846 by friends and associates:

- John Stuart, Mr. Lincoln's first law partner
- Stephen Logan, another law partner
- Joshua Speed, Mr. Lincoln's close friend
- William Herndon, Mr. Lincoln's last law partner and friend for many years
- Mr. Lincoln, age 37
- Mary Todd Lincoln, Mr. Lincoln's wife
- Orville H. Browning, another of Mr. Lincoln's friends

WASHINGTON PANEL: 1861-1865. The Years of Command

The Washington panel focuses on the Civil War. The only recognizable figure is General Ulysses S. Grant. The other figures are soldiers in General Grant's army.

CENTRAL PANEL: "And Now He Belongs to the Ages"

The words "and now he belongs to the ages" were said by Secretary of War Edwin Stanton after President Lincoln died. The figures in this panel represent groups of people, all of whom were affected by Abraham Lincoln's presidency. The two figures on the right are from mythology: Cleo, the muse of history, and Columbia, a symbol for the United States. Columbia is holding a wreath of laurel, the tribute of a nation to its leader.

Activity #6

ABRAHAM LINCOLN: IN HIS OWN WORDS

A Readers Theatre Performance

Invite parents and community members to an evening of Readers Theatre featuring Mr. Abraham Lincoln himself – actually, your entire class roleplaying Mr. Lincoln. In the show, the students take turns reading selections from Mr. Lincoln's speeches, letters, and other writings. Mr. Lincoln was an excellent writer (although he went to school for less than a year) and an eloquent speaker (although he was far from good-looking and his voice was described as high-pitched and reedy).

Readers Theatre is defined by what it is *not* – no memorizing, no props, no sets. Most important, Readers Theatre is *not* the same as reading a play aloud in class. It involves preparation and rehearsal. In the process students will, first of all, come to own the wonderful words Mr. Lincoln wrote. Don't be deterred by the vocabulary, even for the youngest students: if they can memorize the names of dinosaurs or characters in video games, they can learn the vocabulary of 19th Century speech. Secondly, students will learn a lot about the elements of drama: vocal expression, projection, speaking style, and diction.

PROCEDURE

Preparing the script

A staged reading of Lincoln material for 30 students follows the description of this activity. The selections were made in part for what they reveal about Mr. Lincoln and in part to accommodate varied reading and speaking skills. Divide the longer speeches if you need more; cut a few out if you need less, or have a few volunteers take on more than one speech. After you've assigned the parts, put each script in a black binder (the ones that measure 5"x8" are easy for younger hands to hold open). Regarding the quotes, you might explain to students that an elipses (…) means that words have been omitted to make the meaning clearer.

Preparing for rehearsal

Before reading as a group, the students should go over their own lines, making sure they know what the words mean and how to pronounce them. This is a good opportunity to practice dictionary skills. They also need to think about their character's speaking style and voice expression. Yes, they're all playing the part of Mr. Lincoln, but at different times of his life and in different circumstances. A letter written to his wife calls for a very different voice than a formal speech. Students should try out facial expressions and gestures. Remind them that the audience isn't listening only for voices; they will be watching the expressions and gestures the students use.

Rehearsing lines

- Decide whether students are going to sit or stand. If they're standing, don't take for granted they know how: demonstrate standing up straight, arms by your side. If they're sitting, arrange chairs in a line or a semi-circle. Instruct students to keep their feet flat on the ground and sit up straight. Hands and feet should be kept still.

- The actor who speaks steps out of the semi-circle, announces from memory the title of the piece, brings the binder up, opens it, and then holds it with one hand, using the other hand to gesture. Then the actor reads Mr. Lincoln's words. After reading, he or she announces the source of the words and then closes the binder and steps back into place.

- Tell students to hold their scripts so that they can see the words clearly, but to make sure the binders don't hide their faces. When they speak, they should look up often, not just at the script. (Encourage memorization: it's not necessary but it does make for a better performance.)

- Movement can help make the story more effective. A reader has one free hand that can be used to wave, to gesture, to point, and so on. The script itself can be used as a prop. Don't over-direct, but a few gestures and movements can be very effective.

- When you rehearse as a group, make sure you praise the students as often as you make corrections. Model speaking style, diction, and vocal expression. In early rehearsals, stop frequently to address misconceptions.

- Work on voice projection by having a student at the back of the room raise a hand if the voice is not audible.

The crew

Although all students need experience speaking in front of others, some may be distinctly uncomfortable at the prospect of performing for adults. Consider letting them be members of a crew. Crew positions are important, both in professional theater and student theater; moreover, the taste of real responsibility often brings out the best in children.

Stage manager. The stage manager arranges the chairs, or stools, before rehearsal begins. If you keep the scripts at school, it is the stage manager's responsibility to collect and distribute them. While you're rehearsing, the stage manager reads along silently so that you, as director, can watch and listen to the readers without having to look down at the script. If a student misses a cue, the stage manager should read a few of the words so that the actor realizes what he/she should be saying.

Costume crew. A costume crew can be put in charge of keeping the costumes organized and safe before and after the performance. Have them label boxes or paper bags with the students' names.

Musicians. Musicians add immeasurably to the mood of any piece when it's performed, even if they only play before the first speaker and after the last. You can use recorded music or "live" instruments; drums are an especially powerful addition. To keep your musicians busy, let them follow along the rehearsal so that they can decide where and how music can enhance the story.

Costumes

Costumes are important in this Readers Theatre Project: the mass effect of 20-30 Abraham Lincolns on stage will be unforgettable. You have two choices: (1) The Lincolns can be costumed according to the age they are representing, or (2) you can choose to have everyone look like the familiar Lincoln image – the tall hat, black suit, and beard. (Directions for making a hat are included with this lesson. You can make hats as a class project or send the instructions home.)

Beginning & ending

Beginnings and endings are important, and it pays to rehearse them. Have one student introduce the reading by announcing "Abraham Lincoln: In His Own Words." (This can be the same student who closes the reading.) When the final speaker is finished and returns to her/his place, all the readers should freeze for a long moment to break the action. Then they close their scripts, rise, take the hand of the person next to them (right and left) for the company bow. Led by the person in the middle, they all raise hands, bow, and let go of each others' hands, letting their own hands drop down to their sides.

Before the performance

Before an actual performance, go over some "worst case scenarios" with the students:

- If the audience laughs, stop speaking until they can hear again. Don't laugh with them.
- If someone talks in the audience, don't pay attention. (They're being very rude.)
- If someone walks into the room, don't look.
- If you make a mistake, pretend you were doing or saying the right thing. Chances are the audience won't notice.

The performance

Here's one last piece of advice to tell students: have fun and enjoy the applause! Performance is the "payoff" for all the hard work that has led up to producing this event for an audience.

RESOURCES

- Introduce this activity by inviting a Lincoln impersonator to talk with your class. There are hundreds of them across the country, and some may be relatively close to your school. To find one, check with your state or local arts council or historical society.

- Aaron Shepard's *Readers on Stage: Resources for Readers Theatre* is an excellent guide to using Readers Theatre in the classroom. Mr. Shepard's website is www.aaronshep.com.

- This website has good information and many links for teachers interested in producing Readers Theatre projects: www.literacyconnections.com/ReadersTheater.html.

- Several books, written for both adults and young people, use selections from Mr. Lincoln's speeches, letters, and other writings. Here are three good ones:

Holzer, Harold, editor. *Abraham Lincoln, The Writer: A Treasury of His Greatest Speeches and Letters.* Boyds Mills, 2000.

Lang, H.J., editor. *The Wit and Wisdom of Abraham Lincoln.* Stackpole, 2006.

Meltzer, Milton. *Lincoln: In His Own Words.* Harcourt Brace, 1993.

How To Make A Top Hat

The easy way.
Cut out the center of a paper plate, leaving a rim about 2 inches wide. Throw the cut-out away, and paint the rest of the paper plate black. Measure the inside circle. Cut a piece of black construction paper the measurement of the circle, plus 2 inches. Tape this into the circle so that as much as possible sticks out through the top of the plate. Cut one-inch slits in the part that extends underneath the plate. Fold and glue these "tabs" on the underside of the plate.

A better way.
Thorough directions for making a top hat that will look completely authentic are online at www.amtgard-wl.com/library/howtos/how2toph.pdf.

Readers Theatre

Abraham Lincoln

In His Own Words

Speaker 1	**Abraham Lincoln is born** I was born Feb. 12, 1809, in Hardin County, Kentucky. ... My mother, who died in my tenth year, was of a family of the name of Hanks ... My paternal grandfather, Abraham Lincoln, emigrated from ... Virginia, to Kentucky, about 1781 or 2, where, a year or two later, he was killed by Indians, not in battle, but by stealth when he was laboring to open a farm in the forest. **From a short autobiography written December 20, 1859**
Vocabulary	*paternal grandfather – father's father* *by stealth – secretly; sneakily; slyly; silently*

Speaker 2	**A sample of Abraham's written work in school** Abraham Lincoln, his hand and pen. He will be good, but God knows when. **From a rhyme Abraham wrote in his school book**

Speaker 3	**Abraham Lincoln grows up** My father ... moved from Kentucky to what is now Spencer County, Indiana, during my eighth year. We reached our new home about the same time the state came into the Union. It was a wild region with many bears and other wild animals still in the woods. There I grew up. There were some schools so called; but no qualification was ever required of a teacher beyond "readin, writin and cipherin," to the Rule of Three. If a straggler supposed to understand Latin happened to sojourn in the neighborhood, he was looked upon as a wizard. There was absolutely nothing to excite ambition for education. Of course when I came of age I did not know much. Still somehow, I could read, write and cipher to the Rule of Three; but that was all. I have not been to school since. **From a short autobiography written December 20, 1859**
Vocabulary	*qualification – a requirement for employment* *sojourn – travel* *ciphering – arithmetic* *straggler – a person who becomes separated from a group* *Rule of Three – a kind of higher mathematics*

Speaker 4	**Mr. Lincoln's view on the American Revolution** ...Away back in my childhood ... I got ahold of a small book ... Weems' *Life of George Washington*. I remember all the accounts there given of the battlefields and struggles for the liberties of the country ... and I recollect thinking then, boy even though I was, that there must have been something more than common that those men struggled for. **From an address to the Senate of New Jersey, February 21, 1861**
Vocabulary	*accounts – stories, reports* *liberties – freedom* *recollect – remember* *boy even though I was – although I was young* *something more than common – something exceptional and uncommon*

Speaker 5	**Mr. Lincoln as a young man** I was raised to farm work, which I continued till I was twenty-two. At twenty-one I came to Illinois, Macon County. Then I got to New Salem, at that time in Sangamon, now in Menard County, where I remained a year as a sort of clerk in a store. Then came the Black Hawk war; and I was elected a captain of volunteers, a success which gave me more pleasure than any I have had since. I went the campaign, was elated, ran for the legislature the same year (1832), and was beaten – the only time I ever have been beaten by the people. **From a short autobiography written December 20, 1859**
Vocabulary	*elated – very happy* *legislature – an official group of people, usually chosen by election, who have the power to make laws* *went the campaign – stayed in the military*

Speaker 6	**What Mr. Lincoln thought of laboring on the farm** My father taught me to work, but he never taught me to love it. I never did like to work, and I don't deny it. I like to read, tell stories, crack jokes, talk, laugh, anything but work.
Vocabulary	*I don't deny it – I don't say it's not true*

Speaker 7	**Mr. Lincoln's first political announcement** Every man is said to have his peculiar ambition. Whether it be true or not, I can say for one that I have no other so great as that of being truly esteemed of my fellow men, by rendering myself worthy of their esteem. How far I shall succeed in gratifying this ambition, is yet to be developed. I am young and unknown to many of you. I was born and have ever remained in the most humble walks of life. I have no wealthy or popular relations to recommend me. My case is thrown exclusively upon the independent voters of this county. <div align="right">**From a statement of Mr. Lincoln's political beliefs published in the *Sagamo* (Illinois) *Journal*, March 9, 1832**</div>
Vocabulary	*peculiar – belonging to a particular person* *esteemed – admired* *by rendering myself – by making myself* *humble walks of life – poor and unimportant circumstances*

Speaker 8	**Mr. Lincoln as a "military hero"** Did you know I am a military hero? Yes sir; in the days of the Black Hawk war, I fought, bled, and came away. Speaking of General Cass' career reminds me of my own. ... It is quite certain I did not break my sword, for I had none to break; but I bent a musket pretty badly on one occasion. ... If Gen. Cass went in advance of me in picking huckleberries, I guess I surpassed him in charges upon the wild onions. If he saw any live fighting Indians, it was more than I did; but I had a good many bloody struggles with the mosquitoes; and although I never fainted from loss of blood, I can truly say I was often very hungry. <div align="right">**From a speech in the U.S. House of Representatives, July 27, 1848**</div>
Vocabulary	*Musket – a type of gun; a rifle* *Gen. – General* *Black Hawk – chief of a group of Native Americans who fought against the army and Illinois militia (volunteers) in 1832*

Speaker 9	**What did Mr. Lincoln look like?** If any personal description of me is thought desirable, it may be said, I am, in height, six feet, four inches, nearly; lean in flesh, weighing, on an average, one hundred and eighty pounds; dark complexion, with coarse black hair, and gray eyes. **From a short autobiography written December 20, 1859**
Vocabulary	*If a personal description of me is thought desirable – If you want a description of what I look like*

Speaker 10	**Mr. Lincoln and slavery** I am naturally anti-slavery. If slavery is not wrong, nothing is wrong. I cannot remember when I did not so think and feel. **From a letter to Horace Greeley, August 22, 1862**
Vocabulary	*so think and feel – think and believe this is true*

Speaker 11	**Mr. Lincoln marries Mary Todd** Nothing new here, except my marrying, which to me is a matter of profound wonder. **From a letter to a friend, November 11, 1842**
Vocabulary	*profound – deep and sincere*

Speaker 12	**Mr. Lincoln's first important speech** I hate ... the monstrous injustice of slavery itself. I hate it because it deprives our republican example of its just influence in the world. ... Let us re-adopt the Declaration of Independence, and with it, the practices, and policy, which harmonize with it. Let north and south — let all Americans — let all lovers of liberty everywhere — join in the great and good work. If we do this, we shall not only have saved the Union; but we shall have so saved it, as to make, and to keep it, forever worthy of the saving. **From a speech about the Missouri Compromise, October 16, 1854**
Vocabulary	*monstrous – awful, wicked, cruel* *it deprives our republican example of its just influence in the world – this means the United States can't be an example (to other countries) of a government that is fair and good.* *republican – kind of government in which people elect representatives to lead the country and make the laws* *liberty – freedom* *practice and policy – what people choose to do* *Union – The United States* *which harmonize with it – which go along with it*

Speaker 13	**Mr. Lincoln's view of slavery** Dear Speed: You know I dislike slavery, and you fully admit the abstract wrong of if. So far there is no cause of difference. But you say that sooner than yield your legal right to the slave, you would see the Union dissolved ... I acknowledge your rights and my obligations under the Constitution in regard to your slaves. ... In 1841 you and I had together a tedious low-water trip on a steamboat from Louisville to St. Louis. You may remember, as I well do, that ... there were on board ten or a dozen slaves, shackled together with irons. That sight was a continual torment to me; and I see something like it every time I touch the Ohio, or any other slave border. It is hardly fair for you to assume that I have no interest in a thing which has, and continuously exercises, the power of making me miserable. You ought rather to appreciate how much the ... Northern people do crucify their feelings in order to maintain their loyalty to the Constitution and the Union. **From a letter to a friend, August 24, 1855**
Vocabulary	*the abstract wrong of it – it's wrong* *yield – give up* *see the Union dissolved – see the United States broken up* *tedious – boring* *shackled – joined together by chains* *crucify their feelings – try not to think about in an emotional way*

Speaker 14	**An example of Mr. Lincoln's honesty** Dear Sir: I have just received your ... check on Flagg and Savage for twenty-five dollars. You must think I am a high-priced man.... Fifteen dollars is enough for the job. I send you a receipt for fifteen dollars, and return to you a ten-dollar bill. **From a letter written February 23, 1856**

Speaker 15	Mr. Lincoln is nominated for the state senate A house divided against itself cannot stand. I believe this government cannot endure, permanently, half slave and half free. I do not expect the Union to be dissolved – I do not expect the house to fall – but I do expect it will cease to be divided. **From a speech at the state Republican convention, June 16, 1858**
Vocabulary	*endure – last* *Union to be dissolved – the United States to break up* *cease - stop*

64

Speaker 16	**The Lincoln-Douglas debates** . . . [Mr. Douglas] has set about seriously trying to make the impression that when we meet at different places I am literally in his clutches — that I am a poor, helpless, decrepit mouse, and that I can do nothing at all. ... I don't want to quarrel with him — to call him a liar — but when I square up to him I don't know what else to call him. **From the fifth debate with Stephen Douglas, September 18, 1858**
Vocabulary	*decrepit – old and weak* *quarrel – argue*

Speaker 17	**More from the Lincoln-Douglas debates** Let us have faith that might makes right, and in that faith, let us, to the end, dare to do our duty as we understand it. **From an address at the Cooper Union Institute, February 27, 1860**

Speaker 18	**Mr. Lincoln leaves Springfield, Illinois, for Washington, D.C.** No one, not in my situation, can appreciate my feeling of sadness at this parting. To this place, and the kindness of these people, I owe everything. Here I have lived a quarter of a century and have passed from a young to an old man. Here my children have been born and one is buried. **From a farewell address in Springfield, February 11, 1861**
Vocabulary	*parting - leaving*

Speaker 19	**How Mr. Lincoln felt about politics** I have never had a feeling politically that did not spring from the sentiments embodied in the Declaration of Independence. **From an address in Independence Hall, February 22 , 1861**
Vocabulary	*sentiments – thought or idea shared by a group* *embodied in – written in*

Speaker 20	**President warns the Southern states not to leave the Union.** In your hands, my dissatisfied fellow countrymen, and not in mine, is the momentous issue of civil war. The government will not assail you. ... You have no oath registered in Heaven to destroy the government, while I shall have the most solemn one to preserve, protect and defend it. **From the First Inaugural Address, March 4,1861**
Vocabulary	*momentous – extremely important* *assail – attack* *oath registered in Heaven – promise made to God*

Speaker 21	**The Civil War begins** Both parties deprecated war, but one of them would make war rather than let the nation survive; and the other would accept war rather than let it perish. And the war came. **From the Second Inaugural Address, March 4, 1865**
Vocabulary	*both parties – the south and the north* *perish – come to an end; die*

Speaker 22	**President Lincoln on saving the Union** I would save the Union. ... If I could save the Union without freeing any slave, I would do it; and if I could save it by freeing all the slaves, I would do it; and if I could save it by freeing some and leaving others alone, I would also do that. . . . I have here stated my purpose according to my view of official duty; and I intend no modification of my oft-expressed personal wish that all men everywhere could be free. **From a letter to the New York Times published August 25, 1862**
Vocabulary	*modification – change* *oft-expressed – something said over and over again*

Speaker 23	**The Emancipation Proclamation** On the first day of January, in the year of our Lord one thousand eight hundred and sixty-three, all persons held as slaves within any State, or designated part of a state, the people whereof shall then be in rebellion against the United States, shall be then, thenceforward, and forever free. **From The Emancipation Proclamation, January 1, 1863**
Vocabulary	*designated – pointed out* *the people whereof shall then be – the people who are, on that date* *thenceforward – from this point on*

Speaker 24	**Lincoln on the fighting of the war** To General George G. Meade You fought and beat the enemy at Gettysburg; and, of course, to say the least, his loss was as great as yours. He retreated; and you did not, as it seemed to me, pressingly pursue him; but a flood in the river detained him, till, by slow degrees, you were again upon him. You had at least twenty thousand veteran troops directly with you, and as many more raw ones within supporting distance, all in addition to those who fought with you at Gettysburg; while it was not possible that he had received a single recruit; and yet you stood and let the flood run down, bridges be built, and the enemy move away at his leisure, without attacking him. ... I do not believe you appreciate the magnitude of the misfortune involved in Lee's escape. He was within your easy grasp, and to have closed upon him would, in connection with our other late successes, have ended the war. As it is, the war will be prolonged indefinitely. **From a letter to General Meade, July 14, 1863**
Vocabulary	*retreated – moved away from danger by going back the way you came* *pressingly pursue – go after* *detained him – slowed him down* *veteran troops – soldiers who have been in the army a long time* *raw ones –soldiers who have not been in battle* *recruits – new soldiers* *magnitude of the misfortune – how bad it really is* *grasp – take hold of* *to have closed upon him – to catch him* *prolonged – go on longer* *indefinitely – with no end in sight*

Speaker 25	**The Lincoln Family in the White House** My dear Wife. All as well as usual, and no particular trouble any way. I put the money into the Treasury at five per cent, with the privilege of withdrawing it any time upon thirty days' notice. I suppose you are glad to learn this. Tell dear Tad, poor "Nanny Goat" is lost; and Mrs. Cuthbert & I are in distress about it. The day you left, Nanny was found resting herself, and chewing her little cud, on the middle of Tad's bed. But now she's gone! The gardener kept complaining that she destroyed the flowers, till it was concluded to bring her down to the White House. This was done, and the second day she had disappeared, and has not been heard of since. This is the last we know of poor "Nanny." The weather continues dry, and excessively warm here. Nothing very important occurring. **From a letter to Mary Todd Lincoln, August 8, 1863**
Vocabulary	*privilege of withdrawing it – the right to take money out of the bank* *in distress – worried and upset* *till it was concluded – until we decided*

Speaker 26	**Mr. Lincoln and the possibility of peace** Peace does not appear so distant as it did. I hope it will come soon, and come to stay; and so come as to be worth the keeping in all future time. **From a letter to Illinois Republicans, August 26, 1863**
Vocabulary	*distant – far away; far in the future*

Speaker 27	**Mr. Lincoln dedicates a new military cemetery in Pennsylvania**
	Four score and seven years ago our fathers brought forth on this continent a new nation, conceived in Liberty, and dedicated to the proposition that all men are created equal.
	Now we are engaged in a great civil war, testing whether that nation, or any nation so conceived and so dedicated, can long endure. We are met on a great battlefield of that war. We have come to dedicate a portion of that field, as a final resting place for those who here gave their lives that that nation might live. It is altogether fitting and proper that we should do this.
	But, in a larger sense, we cannot dedicate – we cannot consecrate – we cannot hallow this ground. The brave men, living and dead, who struggled here, have consecrated it, far above our poor power to add or detract. The world will little note, nor long remember what we say here, but it can never forget what they did here. It is for us the living, rather, to be dedicated here to the unfinished work which they who fought here have thus far so nobly advanced. It is rather for us to be here dedicated to the great task remaining before us – that from these honored dead we take increased devotion to that cause for which they gave the last full measure of devotion – that we here highly resolve that these dead shall not have died in vain – that this nation, under God, shall have a new birth of freedom – and that government of the people, by the people, for the people, shall not perish from the earth.
	The Gettysburg Address, November 19, 1863
Vocabulary	*Four score and seven years ago – 87 years ago* *conceived – thought up, made* *proposition – idea* *engaged – involved* *endure – last* *dedicate – to set something apart for a special purpose* *consecrate - to call or set apart something as holy or sacred* *detract – take away from* *advanced – pushed forward* *devotion – deep love* *resolve – promise* *died in vain – died for no good reason* *measure – amount; quantity*

Speaker 28	**Women in the Civil War**
	I have never studied the art of paying compliments to women; but I must say that if all that has been said by orators and poets since the creation of the world in praise of women were applied to the women of America, it would not do them justice for their conduct during this war. I will close by saying, God bless the women of America.
	From remarks made in Washington, D.C., March 18, 1864
Vocabulary	*do them justice for – be enough to reward them for* *their conduct – what they did*

Speaker 29	**Mr. Lincoln speaks to some Union soldiers** I am most happy to meet you on this occasion. I understand that it has been your honorable privilege to stand, for a brief period, in the defense of your country, and that now you are on your way to your homes. I congratulate you, and those who are waiting to bid you welcome home from the war; and permit me, in the name of the people, to thank you for the part you have taken in this struggle for the life of the nation. You are soldiers of the Republic, everywhere honored and respected. **From a speech to the 166th Ohio Regiment, August 22, 1864**

Speaker 30	**Mr. Lincoln speaks to some more Union soldiers** I happen temporarily to occupy this big White House. I am living witness that any one of your children may look to come here as my father's child has. **From a speech to the 148th Ohio Regiment, August 31, 1864**

Speaker 31	**Mr. Lincoln writes to the mother of five sons killed in the war** I feel how weak and fruitless must be any words of mine which should attempt to beguile you from the grief of a loss so overwhelming. But I cannot refrain from tendering to you the consolation that may be found in the thanks of the Republic they died to save. I pray that our Heavenly Father may assuage the anguish of your bereavement, and leave you only the cherished memory of the loved and lost, and the solemn pride that must be yours, to have laid so costly a sacrifice upon the altar of Freedom. **From a letter to Mrs. Bixby, November 21, 1864**
Vocabulary	*fruitless – empty; bare* *beguile – to get someone's attention; distract* *refrain from tendering – stop from giving* *consolation – comfort to someone who is sad* *assuage the anguish – help you feel better; ease your suffering* *bereavement – grief caused by a loved one's death* *sacrifice – giving up something valuable*

Speaker 32	**Lincoln's plan for the future after the war** With malice toward none, with charity for all, with firmness in the right as God gives us to see the right, let us strive on to finish the work we are in, to bind up the nation's wounds, to care for him who shall have borne the battle and for his widow and his orphan, to do all which may achieve and cherish a just and lasting peace **From the Second Inaugural Address, March 4, 1865**
Vocabulary	*malice – desire to hurt other people* *charity – love; generosity* *strive on – keep trying* *to bind up – to wrap tightly; to bandage* *borne – carried responsibility for* *achieve – succeed; reach a goal* *cherish – to feel great love or caring for something*

Speaker 33	Abraham Lincoln was shot by John Wilkes Booth on April 12, 1865, while he was in Ford's Theater with his wife and some friends, watching a performance of "Our American Cousin." He died the next day. Edwin M. Stanton, a member of Mr. Lincoln's Cabinet, said, "Now he belongs to the ages."
Vocabulary	*the ages – history*

Activity #7

REMEMBERING MR. LINCOLN: ROLEPLAYS

In this creative writing/drama exercise, students roleplay people Lincoln knew as a way of telling stories about his life, his character, his experiences, and his decisions as President. You might schedule it near the end of your study of Mr. Lincoln or after the class has met someone doing first-person interpretation either at a museum or as a visitor to the school.

PROCEDURE

Introducing the lesson

Tell students that after President Lincoln was assassinated, his good friend and law partner, William Herndon, began to collect stories about his life, planning to write a biography. He contacted virtually everyone Lincoln knew, including family members, clients of his law firm, neighbors, former employers, people who worked for him, associates in Washington and Springfield. His collection grew to thousands upon thousands of pages of letters, notes, newspapers, interviews, and more. He did eventually write a biography, but the primary source material itself is much more interesting. In 1998, some of it was published as *Herndon's Informants: Letters, Interviews, and Statements about Abraham Lincoln.*

Explain to students the difference between a primary and a secondary source:
  - A **primary source** is a document (letters, manuscripts, diaries, newspapers, speeches, interviews, journals, maps, documents, notes, photographs) created at the time historical events occurred. Primary sources provide firsthand evidence of historical events.

  - A **secondary source** is research written after studying primary sources. Most non-fiction reference books are secondary sources (e.g., textbooks, biographies, history books).

In this exercise, students will reproduce what might have been primary source material.

Conducting the lesson

Writing a memoir

Assign each student a character (or have them select their own from the list on the following page). Tell them their characters knew Abraham Lincoln personally at some time in his life. Mr. Herndon has asked each of them to write down their memories and any impressions of Mr. Lincoln they might have. Essentially, they're going to write a "memoir" from the point of view of an historical character.

Instructions for the memoir

- The memoir should focus on an event only known to your character. In other words, don't repeat details well known to everyone (e.g., "I remember that Abraham Lincoln was born in a log cabin").
- Write in first person (e.g., "I traveled on the flatboat with Abraham").
- Write in the past tense (e.g., "I went to school with Lincoln").
- The story must be true, but you will probably have to make up some of the small details.
- Write informally, as if you're talking to the other person.

Spend several days on research and writing. After students have finished a first draft, have each of them tell a story to a partner. Their revision can be based, in part, on what the partner found most interesting.

Performing a monologue of the memoir

After the memoirs are finished, invite students to roleplay their characters and read their memoirs to the class. Encourage them to dress in costumes and use props. The proper music can enhance a performance as well. (It's a good idea to have few things on hand for students who aren't able to bring things from home.)

Let students know that role-playing is not the same thing as reading. It takes the kind of preparation that a professional movie actor might do before filming begins. Here are some tips:

- Students should read their memoirs aloud to themselves several times, taking care to pronounce words clearly and distinctly.
- They should experiment with the character's speaking style: does the character have an accent or speak in a funny voice? Can students use their voices to show how old their characters are?
- Students should also experiment with vocal expression. Is the character sad or excited? If the memoir includes a funny story, how can voice be used to relay humor?
- They should try out facial expressions and gestures. A few gestures and movements can be very effective.
- Remind students that when they read, they should hold their scripts with one hand, leaving the other free to gesture. Also, they should look up often, not just at the script. (If they have rehearsed well and are familiar with the script, they won't lose the place.)

Concluding the lesson

Encourage students to come up with costumes for performance. The roleplays can be part of a public celebration of Abraham Lincoln's life to which you invite parents and other students. You also might consider collecting the memoirs into a binder, much as William Herndon's material was bound into a book. It'll be a good source of information for next year's class!

RESOURCES

A sample memoir and a list of "starters" is included with this lesson.

Several books and websites useful for research are listed in Chapter Five. These two are particularly useful:

Mr. Lincoln and Friends – www.mrlincolnandfriends.org

Noting that Mr. Lincoln "had a talent for friendship," this site separates the people Mr. Lincoln knew into ten categories: boys, lawyers, journalists, politicians, members of Congress, Cabinet members, Army officers, sons, preachers, and women. Each link includes stories and quotes which make the relationships very real. (Suitable for older students.)

Spartacus Educational – www.spartacus.schoolnet.co.uk/USAlincoln.htm

This eclectic British website has a very nice interactive biography of President Lincoln. Good for student research.

CHARACTER STARTERS FOR MEMOIRS

1. My name is Sarah Lincoln. I'm Abraham's sister, and I remember when we had to walk four miles just to get to school.

2. My name is Austin Gollaher. I was Abraham Lincoln's best friend, and once I saved him from drowning in the creek.

3. My name is Caleb Hazel and I taught school in Kentucky. I never met a boy as eager to learn as young Abraham Lincoln.

4. My name is Dennis Hanks. I'm Abraham's cousin, and I remember when we were left all alone in Indiana while Abraham's father went to Kentucky to marry.

5. My name is Matilda Johnston. I'm Abraham's step-sister, and I remember some of the pranks Abraham and my brother used to pull when they were teenagers.

6. My name is Josiah Crawford. I remember lending a book to Abraham once.

7. My name is Allen Gentry. Abraham and I took a flatboat on a thousand-mile trip down the Ohio and Mississippi Rivers when we were 19 years old.

8. My name is Jack Armstrong. I used to be the toughest person in New Salem until Abraham Lincoln came along.

9. My name is Joshua Speed. I was Abraham's best friend. I remember meeting him for the first time in the grocery store in New Salem.

10. My name is Royal Clary, and I served in the militia with Abraham Lincoln during the Black Hawk War. In fact, the boys and I elected him our captain.

11. My name is Billy Herndon. I was Abraham's law partner and good friend. We shared an office for years, and I remember he used to keep all his important papers in his hat.

12. My name is Stephen Douglas. I wanted to be the senator for Illinois ... and so did Abraham Lincoln. We had some pretty good debates with each other.

13. My name is Edwin Stanton. I served Mr. Lincoln as his Secretary of War, but I disagreed with many of the things he did as President.

14. My name George McClellan. I was the first general of the Army when the Civil War started. I wanted to wait until the troops were fully trained, but Mr. Lincoln kept pushing me to attack.

15. My name is Frederick Douglass. I am a writer, a speaker, and a former slave who escaped from the South. I remember the first time I went to the White House to meet with President Lincoln.

16. My name is Edward Everett. I gave a speech at Gettysburg on the same day President Lincoln did.

17. My name is Ulysses S. Grant. I was the last general of the Union army during the Civil War. President Lincoln had a great deal of faith in me.

18. My name is John Hay. I was Mr. Lincoln's assistant when he was President, and I saw how he changed during the four long years of the Civil War.

19. My name is Major Henry Rathbone. I was seated next to Mr. and Mrs. Lincoln in Ford's Theater when that crazy actor fired a gun at him.

20. My name is Mary Surratt, and I despised Abe Lincoln. I was part of John Wilkes Booth's conspiracy to assassinate him and members of his government.

21. My name is Mary Todd Lincoln. I was Mr. Lincoln's wife. There have been so many tragedies in my life, and I don't know if I can ever get over all that has happened to me.

Sarah Bush Johnston Lincoln
A character memoir monologue

It's well known that Lincoln liked to read and was very fond of his stepmother. This memoir was developed from two more bits of historical information: (1) Sarah Johnston married Abraham Lincoln's father in 1819, when Abraham was ten, and (2) she brought several books with her when she came to Indiana with her new husband.

My name is Sarah Johnston – but most people call me Sally. I married Thomas Lincoln in 1819 and came to Indiana to be Abraham's stepmother. I remember when I first laid eyes on that boy and his sister Sarah, poor mites. They'd been on their own for awhile. They were sitting on a rock outside the cabin, dressed in filthy rags and shivering. And that cabin! No door, no window, no floor but dirt. It was filthy inside, and there wasn't a thing to eat. Well, I've never been afraid of hard work and I got straight to it. Sarah, she was so sweet, but oh, I remember how Abraham pitched a fit. He was ten years old then, tall as some of the men already, but no, he wasn't going help unload the wagon, and no, he wasn't going to have a bath, and no, he wasn't going to do this, and no, he wasn't going to do that. "You're not my mother," he said. "I don't have to listen to you!"

Well, I just laughed and told him he and I could have a talk whenever he was ready. So he sat on a stump and looked out in the woods. But he kept peeking back at us, as we unloaded the wagon, and I saw his eyes get big when I brought out my books. I loved to read, always did, and I had a fair library back then, not what you usually see on the frontier – I had a biography of President Washington, a book of Aesop's Fables, a great adventure story called Robinson Crusoe and another one called Pilgrim's Progress. And The Arabian Nights. That was my favorite. I was telling Sarah about stories in the Arabian Nights, and she kept looking over at her brother, motioning him to join us but trying not to let me see.

I just said, "If we can get all this squared-away before nightfall, I'll read you a story about the princess who tricked an evil king." Pretty soon, Abraham began inching his way over to us; and before long he was working as hard as everyone else. Well, we had that wagon unloaded lickety-split, and then Abraham carried bucket after bucket full of water from the creek for our baths. When we were finished, we sat down together, and we read as much as we could before it got dark. Thomas fussed a bit, but I told him we needed to make time for reading. My, you should have seen Abraham grin from ear to ear when he heard that. I swear, I never knew a child who loved books as much as Abraham.

Activity #8

THE LINCOLN-DOUGLAS DEBATES: ROLEPLAYS

Abraham Lincoln and Stephen Douglas competed against each other for election to the Illinois Senate. In 1858, they agreed to a series of seven debates to be held throughout Illinois. Mr. Lincoln lost the election. However, the debates attracted national attention, and the new Republican party nominated Abraham Lincoln as their first candidate for President largely because of his eloquence and his position on the issue of slavery. The format remains today as the standard for competition and classroom debates on current issues.

In this activity, the basic Lincoln-Douglas debate format is altered so that teams of students can assume the roles of Abraham Lincoln and Stephen Douglas to debate the spread of slavery into the territories.

PROCEDURE

Introducing the topic

Ask the students about the key issues in a recent election. If you choose the 2008 presidential election, for example, the key issues were the economy, the war in Iraq, global climate change, the energy crisis, illegal immigration, and health care.

What were the issues in 1858, the year Abraham Lincoln debated Stephen Douglas? One issue dominated Illinois politics – and national politics – at the time: slavery. Mr. Douglas believed that territories wanting to become states should decide for themselves whether slavery was legal. Mr. Lincoln thought that the national government should not allow slavery in any new states. Although he was adamantly opposed to slavery, he was not an abolitionist because he didn't think the government, under the Constitution, had the power to declare slavery illegal. He thought that, given time, slavery in the South would end. (Some of the leaders in the Confederacy felt the same way.)

The debate format

The classic Lincoln-Douglas debate is between two people, each of whom represents one side (Affirmative or Negative) of an issue. Explain to the students that the Affirmative group is *for* the statement, and the Negative group is *against* it. The issue is a question or statement (e.g., "Slavery should not be permitted in new territories acquired by the United States").

Adapt the format to involve more students by dividing the class into groups of five students.

Assign students in each group one of the following roles:

- The **moderator** (Team A) calls the debaters to order and introduces the team members and announces the topic to be debated.
- The **timekeeper** (Team N) keeps track of time limits.
- The **lead debater** (Teams A and N) presents the main points of the argument the team has assembled.
- The **questioner** (Teams A and N) asks questions about the other team's position.
- The **responder** (Teams A and N) responds to questions posed by the other team.
- The **closer** (Teams A and N) closes the debate by summarizing the team's position.

Give each group time to research their positions. (You can use the excerpts that are included with this lesson or have them research on their own.) Remind them that in this exercise they are presenting the positions held by Mr. Douglas and Mr. Lincoln, so their own opinions should not enter into the debate. Have them summarize their main points (3-5) on a sheet of paper to be turned in at the close of the debate.

Conducting the debate

Here's how the debate should go (you may wish to adjust times):

Time	Person	Action
	Moderator	Calls the debate to order, introduces participants and announces the statement to be debated
	Timekeeper	Alerts speakers when their time has expired
6 minutes	Lead Debater (Affirmative)	Presents the main points of the team's position, supported with evidence and reason
3 minutes	Questioner (Negative)	Cross-examines affirmative points
6 minutes	Lead Debater (Negative)	Presents the main points of the team's position, supported with evidence and reason
3 minutes	Questioner (Affirmative)	Cross-examines negative points
4 minutes	Responder (Affirmative)	Restates position, responding to cross-examination
4 minutes	Responder (Negative)	Restates position, responding to cross-examination
3 minutes	Closer (Affirmative team)	Summarizes main points of the team's position
3 minutes	Closer (Negative team)	Summarizes main points of the team's position

Concluding the debate

As two teams face off in a debate, the rest of the students are transformed into the citizens of Illinois (voters of the time were all male, of course) who will have to decide who they will they vote for, based on the debates. Again, they should not be voting their own opinions. If asked, they should be able to explain why they chose to vote as they did.

RESOURCES

Find out more about the historic debates:

The Lincoln-Douglas Debates of 1858
Lincoln Home
www.nps.gov/liho/historyculture/debates.htm

The site includes a map of the debate sites and the speeches given by both Mr. Lincoln and Mr. Douglas.

This online lesson tweaks the all-class Lincoln-Debate format in several useful ways:

Stage a Debate: A Primer for Teachers
Education World
www.educationworld.com/a_lesson/03/lp304-01.shtml

More information about classroom debates is available online:

Sources for Classroom Debates
Education World
www.educationworld.com/a_lesson/lesson/lesson304b.shtml

LINCOLN-DOUGLAS DEBATES

What Mr. Douglas said:

I hold that Illinois had a right to abolish and prohibit slavery as she did, but I hold that Kentucky had the same right to continue and protect slavery that Illinois has to abolish it. I hold that New York had as much right to abolish slavery, as Virginia has to continue it. I hold that each and every State of this Union is a sovereign power, with the right to do as it pleases on this question of slavery. ...

Why should Illinois be at war with Missouri, or Kentucky with Ohio, or Virginia with New York, merely because their institutions differ? Our fathers intended that these institutions should differ. Our fathers knew that the South and the North, so far apart – differing in climate and production, had different interests requiring different institutions. This doctrine of uniformity, of Mr. Lincoln's making all of them conform alike, is new doctrine, never dreamed of by Washington or Madison, or the framers of the Constitution. Mr. Lincoln and the Republican Party set themselves up as wiser than those who made the government.

This government has flourished for seventy years upon the principle of popular sovereignty, recognizing the right of each State to do as it pleases. Under that principle, we have grown up from three or four millions to about thirty millions of people. Under that principle, we have crossed the Allegheny Mountains, and filled up the whole Northwest, turning the prairie into a garden, building up cities, and towns, and churches, and schools, and spreading civilization and Christianity where before there was nothing but savage barbarism. Under that principle, we have become from a feeble nation the most powerful nation on the face of the earth. If we still only obey that principle we can go forward, increasing in territory, increasing in power, in strength and glory, until the Republic of America shall be the North star that shall guide the friends of freedom throughout the civilized world. Then, my friends, why can we not adhere to that great principle of self-government upon which our institutions were originally made?

I believe that this new doctrine preached by Mr. Lincoln and this Abolition party would dissolve the Union. They try to array all the Northern states in one body against the South, inviting a sectional war of the Free states against the Slave states – Northern states against Southern states, to last until the one or the other shall be driven to the wall.

From the First Debate, Ottawa, Illinois, August 21, 1858

What Mr. Lincoln said:

I suggest that the difference of opinion, reduced to its lowest terms, is no other than the difference between the men who think slavery a wrong and those who do not think it wrong. The Republican party thinks it wrong – we think it is a moral, a social and a political wrong. We think it as a wrong not confining itself merely to the persons or the States where it exists, but that it is a wrong in its tendency, to say the least, that extends itself to the existence of the whole nation. Because we think it wrong, we propose a course of policy that shall deal with it as a wrong. We deal with it as with any other wrong, insofar as we can prevent its growing any larger, and so deal with it that in the run of time there may be some promise of an end to it. We have a due regard to the actual presence of it amongst us and the difficulties of getting rid of it in any satisfactory way, and all the Constitutional obligations thrown about it. I suppose that in reference both to its actual existence in the nation, and to our Constitutional obligations, we have no right at all to disturb it in the states where it exists, and we profess that we have no more inclination to disturb it than we have the right to do it. ...

Judge Douglas asks you, "Why cannot the institution of slavery, or rather, why cannot the nation, part slave and part free, continue as our fathers made it forever?" In the first place, I insist that our fathers did not make this nation half slave and half free, or part slave and part free. I insist that they found the institution of slavery existing here. They did not make it so, but they left it so because they knew of no way to get rid of it at that time. When Judge Douglas undertakes to say that as a matter of choice the fathers of the government made this nation part slave and part free, he assumes what is historically a falsehood. More than that; when the fathers of the government cut off the source of slavery by the abolition of the slave trade, and adopted a system of restricting it from the new territories where it had not existed, I maintain that they placed it where they understood, and all sensible men understood, it was in the course of ultimate extinction; and when Judge Douglas asks me why it cannot continue as our fathers made it, I ask him why he and his friends could not let it remain as our fathers made it? ...

There is no reason in the world why the Negro is not entitled to all the rights enumerated in the Declaration of Independence – the right of life, liberty, and the pursuit of happiness. I hold that he is as much entitled to these as the white man.

From the Sixth Debate, Quincy, Illinois, October 13 1858

Activity #9

THE FIRST READING OF
THE EMANCIPATION PROCLAMATION

Art Analysis

The First Reading of the Emancipation Proclamation, a painting made by Francis Carpenter in 1863, hangs today in the United States Capitol. By analyzing the painting, students can learn more about how slavery was regarded in Mr. Lincoln's government and why Mr. Lincoln made the choice only to free slaves in the states that had seceded from the Union.

Introducing the activity

Share the following with students:

> In the middle of 1862, things did not look good for either the Union or for Abraham Lincoln's presidency (1861-1865). What many had thought would be a short war that would lead to the South rejoining the Union had turned into a bloody conflict with no end in sight. The Confederate Army had been successful. France and Britain were getting close to agreeing that the Confederate States of America was a separate nation. On July 22, Lincoln met with his Cabinet on the second floor of the White House. He told them that he had written a document that would free many of the slaves in the South. He asked them for their opinion. The response was divided, but Lincoln had already made up his mind to sign the proclamation. He followed advice that he should wait to tell the public until the Union Army had won a battle. He did not want Americans to think that he was freeing the slaves because the Union cause was desperate. In September 1862, with a win at the battle of Antietam, Lincoln told the nation that he would officially sign the Emancipation Proclamation in 100 days — on January 1, 1863. On New Year's Day, after greeting hundreds of visitors at the annual White House reception, Lincoln went upstairs to his office. With a shaking hand, he signed the proclamation. From that moment, the war had two aims: to preserve the Union and to fight for freedom. Lincoln said he never "felt more certain that I was doing right, than I do in signing this paper." (From www.whitehousehistory.org.)

Tell students that the Emancipation Proclamation did not free all the slaves in the United States. It was a wartime measure only. Slavery wasn't totally outlawed until the Thirteenth Amendment to the Constitution, which was proposed by Congress on January 31, 1865, and formally adopted on December 6, 1865, when it had been ratified by three-quarters of the states, as required by the Constitution.

Why do students think Mr. Lincoln, who was adamantly opposed to slavery, chose only to free the slaves in the states that had seceded from the Union? (The border states, which had stayed in the Union, were slave states; Mr. Lincoln didn't want to lose their support in the war.

Freeing the slaves in the South meant that the South lost a valuable source of free labor and also meant that the Union armies could enlist more men.)

PROCEDURE

The First Step: Responding to the Painting

Show students a copy of the painting. (Look online or make copies of the illustration in Chapter Five.) Without telling them the title, have them answer this question in their journals: *What is going on in this picture?*

The Second Step: Objective Observations

Divide students into four groups. Assign each group one of the following parts of speech: noun, verb, adverb and adjective. Each group's task is to come up with words that describe aspects of the painting using only their assigned part of speech. *(HINT: Construct your groups in such a way so that students with particular talents in language arts are in the adjective and adverb groups.)* Here are some of the words they might come up with:

> **Nouns**: men, Abraham Lincoln, papers, quill pen, map books, paintings, chairs and table, fireplace
> **Verbs**: sit, stand, read, stare, think
> **Adverbs and adjectives**: well-dressed, messy, formal, tired, calmly, seriously, solemn

As the groups share their words, write them on the board, and then form some sentences using them (e.g., *The tired, well-dressed men sit around a table as Abraham Lincoln reads from papers*).

Now give them some more information about the objects in the painting.

- The framed painting above the mantelpiece is of Andrew Jackson, who was president from 1828-1836.
- The document on the table is the U.S. Constitution.
- The men are all members of President Lincoln's Cabinet (that is, his advisors). From left, they are Secretary of War Edward Stanton (seated), Secretary of the Treasury Salmon P. Chase, President Lincoln, Secretary of the Navy Gideon Welles, Secretary of the Interior Caleb B. Smith, Postmaster General Montgomery Blair, Attorney General Edward Bates, and Secretary of State William Seward (seated in front of the table).

The Third Step: Subjective Observations

Symbols.
Ask why the artist included the objects he did. Why are there two documents in the painting (the Constitution and the Proclamation)? Why is there a painting of Andrew Jackson, of all the Presidents? (He was a staunch supporter of the Union and had dealt with South Carolina's threat of secession from the Union in 1828-1830.) Why are there

so many books? Was it just because they were there in the room, or do books serve another purpose? (In the 19th Century when not everyone could read, books indicated an educated person.) The map reminds viewers that it was America's destiny to spread across the continent and that the prevention of the extension of slavery into new territories had been an important struggle of the previous decades.

Composition.

What do students think is happening in the painting? What is the relationship between the men? They know, because of the title, that Mr. Lincoln is sharing the proclamation he has written with his Cabinet members for the first time. At this point, they should include their personal feelings and opinions. Can they tell what the individuals are feeling (e.g., tired, bored, proud) from their expressions? Do all the men in the picture get along with President Lincoln? Are they all in support of President Lincoln's decision to free the slaves in the states that seceded only? Are they in favor of it at all?

After some discussion, tell students that the artist said his intention was to show Mr. Lincoln testing how the members of his Cabinet feel about slavery. Not everyone in the North supported the Emancipation Proclamation. Some people saw it as too little, too late. Here's what the members of the Cabinet thought:

- Secretary of War Stanton saw the Proclamation as a military act, designed to weaken the South by taking away its free labor, and also as a way to bring more soldiers into the Union army.
- Secretary of the Treasury Chase was a longtime opponent of slavery and was very supportive of the Proclamation.
- Secretary of the Navy Welles strongly supported the Emancipation Proclamation.
- Secretary of the Interior Smith was not convinced it was a good idea. He was concerned about the voters' reactions.
- Postmaster General Montgomery Blair also opposed the Emancipation Proclamation because he believed the voters would not be in favor of it.
- Attorney General Bates doubted that the Proclamation was constitutional. He opposed civil and political equality for African-Americans.
- Secretary of State Seward strongly supported the Emancipation Proclamation.

How did the artist show these varying attitudes in the painting? (Postmaster General Blair and Secretary Smith, who oppose the Emancipation Proclamation, are standing in the back; they look very uncomfortable. Attorney General Bates, who thinks it is unconstitutional, is seated, but he is removed from the others. All the others are seated, and they look a bit more comfortable. Secretary Chase is standing. His crossed arms give the impression that he is ready for a battle.)

Light.

Ask students to point out what parts of the painting seem lighter than others. If so, why has the artist chosen to do this? (The region around Mr. Lincoln is lighter. Light is often used symbolically to indicate truth and righteousness.)

The Fourth Step: Reflection

Ask students if they can describe the tone or mood of this painting. (Expect them to use words such as "serious" or "important.") How do students think the artist himself felt about slavery and the Emancipation Proclamation? What evidence in the painting suggests their response?

FURTHER EXPLORATION

Have students go through this process with different paintings or photos from Lincoln's lifetime. A good choice for photo analysis is *Lincoln on Battlefield at Antietam,* found at www.artsedge. org/content/3901.

RESOURCES

These websites may be useful:

http://en.wikipedia.org/wiki/Image:Emancipation_proclamation.jpg
> Information and a large image of *First Reading of the Emancipation Proclamation*

http://en.wikipedia.org/wiki/Image:EmancipationProclamation.jpg
> Photographic image of the "Proclamation of Emancipation" document

http://memory.loc.gov/ammem/alhtml/almintr.html
> Library of Congress *American Memory* website
> Original documents relating to the Emancipation Proclamation
> Timeline
> Mr. Lincoln's handwritten first draft of the Emancipation Proclamation

Activity #10

DRAW A POLITICAL CARTOON

Political cartooning in America has been around since the Revolution. Benjamin Franklin was one of the first political cartoon artists in the U.S. He drew a picture of a snake cut into eight parts, labeled each part with a name of one of the states (colonies), and added the caption "Join or Die." By the time of the Civil War, political cartoons appeared regularly in newspapers.

Conduct this activity after students have learned about Mr. Lincoln's decisions during the election of 1860 and in the Civil War.

PROCEDURE

Introducing the activity

Tell students that – like the cartoons in comic books – political or editorial cartoons tell a story in pictures. But they do more: a political cartoon can explain a complicated situation, and it can state a very strong opinion. Political cartoons can make the viewer laugh, but they can also be extremely serious in their intent.

Conducting the activity

Present-day political cartoons

> Collect several examples of political cartoons that address current events. Try to find some that express opposing opinions. Your local newspaper may be your best source, but you can find current cartoons with interpretations online at www.cagle.com/teacher.

> As you show each cartoon, talk to students about the fact that bias is acceptable in a political cartoon which, like an editorial, is supposed to present the artist's opinion. Also address *caricature* (exaggeration of personal characteristics), *personification* (attributing human characteristics to animals or objects), and *symbols* (something that represents something else). Point out examples of each in the cartoons.

> Check to see how well students can interpret a political cartoon they haven't seen before. Having background knowledge that gives them an appropriate frame of reference is essential. Divide the class into groups of two or three and give each group a political cartoon to analyze. (All groups can use the same cartoon). Have them complete one *Political Cartoon Analysis* worksheet provided with this lesson for each cartoon they use.

Political cartoons in Mr. Lincoln's time

Share with students some of the cartoons that lampooned Mr. Lincoln. (You can locate political cartoons online or use those included with this lesson.) Have them complete a separate *Political Cartoon Analysis* worksheet for each political cartoon they analyze.

Creating a political cartoon

Instruct students to decide on an issue or situation in Mr. Lincoln's own time and draw a political cartoon about it. Emphasize that you're not looking for artistic excellence, but rather how well they use the format to convey an idea or opinion.

Here are some possible cartoon topics:

- Mr. and Mrs. Lincoln were criticized for allowing their children to "run wild" in the White House. Draw a cartoon showing Tad and Willie as wild beasts tearing through the living room. Include the Lincoln parents' reactions, as well as the reaction from a visiting dignitary.

- Mr. Lincoln ran against Stephen Douglas for the presidency in 1860. Draw the election as a horserace, with Mr. Lincoln's long legs putting him in the lead.

Concluding the activity

Allow students to share their cartoons with others in the class, and post them on a bulletin board or in the hallway for others to enjoy.

RESOURCES

Find a gallery of more political cartoons at the Lilly Library, University of Indiana website:
www.indiana.edu/~liblilly/cartoon/civil.html.

POLITICAL CARTOON ANALYSIS

IMAGES	*WORDS*
List objects or people in the cartoon.	*Write the cartoon caption and/or title.* *Are any of the characters speaking?* *What other words are in the cartoon?*
Are objects/people on your list symbols? What do they mean?	*What words or phrases are most significant? Why?* *List adjectives describing emotions for the image.*

IMAGES & WORDS
Describe the action taking place in the cartoon.
Explain the overall message of the cartoon.

POLITICAL CARTOONS

STORMING THE CASTLE

Storming the Castle, 1860

This cartoon pictures the four candidates for president (Mr. Lincoln, John Bell, Stephen Douglas, and John C. Breckinridge), along with President Buchanan at the window. Mr. Lincoln is costumed as a "Wide-Awake," a political club of the time. He carries a lantern (symbol of truth) and a sharpened rail.

The Writing of the Emancipation Proclamation, 1863

A cartoon from the Confederacy. The artist has filled Mr. Lincoln's room with images of the devil, as if to suggest the devil is influencing the writing of the Proclamation that freed the slaves in Rebel states.

THE "RAIL SPLITTER" AT WORK REPAIRING THE UNION.

The "Rail Splitter" at Work Repairing the Union, 1865

The man on top of the globe, sewing the states back together is Vice-President Andrew Johnson, from the Southern state of Tennessee. Mr. Lincoln props up the world with a split rail (he used to split logs with an axe as a young man).

Chapter Three

Good Ideas for Learning About Mr. Lincoln

1. Celebrate

Host a "Happy Birthday, Mr. Lincoln" party every February 12. Invite parents and community members.

2. Lincoln Look-alikes

Sponsor an Abraham Lincoln look-alike contest. Take it a step further and require contestants to choose one of Mr. Lincoln's better-known speeches to perform for an audience.

3. Art Exhibit #1

Hold an Abraham Lincoln Art Contest. Challenge students school-wide to create their own drawings or portraits of Mr. Lincoln. Set up categories (e.g., portraits, Mr. Lincoln in Action, Mr. Lincoln and Friends). Prizes can be Lincolniana (e.g., pencils, keychains, pennies or anything with Mr. Lincoln's face on it).

4. Art Exhibit #2

Challenge older students to come up with artworks on a specific theme that relates to Mr. Lincoln (e.g., "Freedom, equality, and opportunity"). Making it a contest will encourage more submissions.

5. Images of Abraham Lincoln

Have students collect as many different images of Lincoln as they can find for an exhibit. Eighth graders can stick to the historic photos, but younger children can collect all kinds of images, including stamps, money, statues, toys, souvenirs and more.

6. Create a Trivia Game

In your computer lab, bookmark some of the websites listed in the resources section (Chapter 5). Send the students, in groups or two or three, to a computer and tell them they are to find information on Abraham Lincoln that they think is important for others to know. Each group should come up with at least five good questions and answers. Young students can create simple questions based on facts, but encourage older ones to come up with questions that reflect cause-and-effect relationships or analyze historical events by using a point system (more difficult questions earn more points).

Pass out some index cards, and tell them to write the question on one side of the card and the answer on the other. Collect the cards, shuffle them, and use them for any kind of quiz game (e.g., jeopardy, quick recall). *NOTE: If computer access is difficult, you can also do this activity with print resources.*

Here's one way to play:
Divide the class into two teams according to some predetermined criterion, which may be nonsensical (e.g., students wearing blue against those wearing other colors, students who have dogs against those with cats or no pets, etc.). Each group is to form a line. The two people at the head of the lines will compete against each other. Read one of the questions.

Students have five seconds to answer. The person who gives the correct answer first stays in line; the other sits down. If there is a tie, or if neither knows the answer, read another question. The person who knows the right answer then competes against the next person in the other line. Continue until all the people in one line sit down. The other line wins.

7. The Election of 1860 Revisited

Divide the class into four groups, and assign each group one of the four candidates for President in 1860: *Mr. Lincoln*, who wanted to keep the Union together but opposed any extension of slavery; *Stephen Douglas*, who thought that states should be able to decide for themselves whether or not slavery was legal; *John Breckinridge*, who supported slavery; and *John Bell*, who thought the problem of slavery might go away if it was ignored. Each group is to prepare a presidential campaign, with speeches, flyers, songs, and whatever else they come up with. Ask for four volunteers to portray the candidates and make presentations to another class. Hold a vote. Who wins?

Ask students why they voted as they did. If students didn't vote for Mr. Lincoln, why not? Based on the results of the voting, discuss the changes to the United States in the 150 years following the election. What would the United States be like now if Mr. Lincoln hadn't won the election?

See an online exhibition of Mr. Lincoln and the media on the History Now website:
  www.historynow.org/12_2005/interactive.html
Information on the election is available at the History Central website:
  www.multied.com/elections/1860.html

8. The Election of 1864 Revisited

Mr. Lincoln was re-elected President in 1864, despite the fact that the U.S. was involved in a terrible civil war. Of course, the men in the Southern states couldn't vote – and neither could any women in the North or the South. Do students think the election might have turned out differently if women had been allowed to vote? Ask them to explain their reasoning.

Ask students how campaigning in 1864 might differ from campaigning in the 21st Century. (If they don't suggest television advertising, bring it up.) Divide the class into groups of three or four: each group's task is to come up with one-minute television ad encouraging citizens to vote for Mr. Lincoln. Make sure that each commercial includes substantive information (e.g., his platform, his political philosophy). Videotape the ads and share them with the class.

9. Introducing Mr. Lincoln

Invite a Lincoln re-enactor to your class. To find one, check with your state or local arts council or historical society.

10. To Tell the Truth

Play a game of "To Tell the Truth" with three volunteer Lincolns on the panel and you as the moderator. Assign all students the same short biography, either print (e.g., *Meet Abraham*

Lincoln by Barbara Carey) or online. Make sure the three Lincoln impersonators study it thoroughly. Questions will come from the audience. One of the Lincolns should stick to the truth, but the other two should make small changes when they are responding to questions. You can find a script for this by Googling "To Tell the Truth: Abraham Lincoln," but it's more fun, and the students will learn more, if you and they set it up together using their ideas.

11. You Were There: The Assassination of President Abraham Lincoln

Twenty-five documents relating to the assassination of President Lincoln are available in a gallery through the Library of Congress American Memory website, http://memory.loc.gov/ammem/alhtml/almintr.html. Also included is a brief summary and a timeline of the assassination and its aftermath which puts the documents in context. Print out the documents or have students examine them online. Make sure they understand the difference between a primary and a secondary source (see page 71). In response to what they see, each of them is to create some sort of document to add to the collection (e.g., a drawing, a poster, an invitation, a painting, a newspaper or journal article, a letter).

12. Mr. Lincoln in Context: Understanding Slavery

An excellent lesson on understanding slavery in the 19th Century is available through the Library of Congress American Memory website, http://memory.loc.gov/learn/lessons/psources/pshome.html. This lesson introduces students to primary sources – what they are, their great variety, how they can be analyzed – and then applies these techniques to analyze documents about slavery.

13. The Gettysburg Address and Read-Write-Think

The Gettysburg Address is very short, but with its 267 words President Lincoln managed to honor the sacrifice of the soldiers and remind Americans why the war was being fought. Ask a student who reads with good expression to read the speech aloud. Then have students answer the following questions, either orally or on paper.

1. Who is the speaker of the text?
2. What is the occasion of the speech?
3. Who is the intended audience?
4. What is the purpose of the speech?
5. What is the subject matter of the speech?
6. What is the tone of the speech?
7. What, in your opinion, is the most memorable idea or phrase from the speech?

Students can use the same technique to analyze any speeches or writings by Mr. Lincoln.

14. The Gettysburg Address and Textual Analysis

Print a copy of the Gettysburg Address and cut it into sentences. Divide students into pairs, and give each pair a sentence. Each pair is to figure out what the sentence means and present their findings to the class as a whole.

15. The Bear Hunt

Read the poem "The Bear Hunt," which Mr. Lincoln wrote in 1844 about an episode from his youth in Indiana. (It could be imagined; one of the limitations of history is that we can't know for sure.) A Language Arts class might want to analyze the poem, noting its literary techniques (simile, rhyming pattern, metaphor, onomatopoeia, personification, etc.). It can also be used to springboard a discussion about differences between Indiana when Lincoln was a boy and now (i.e., Have you seen any bears lately?). A copy of the poem can be found at this website, www.theatlantic.com/doc/192502/lincoln-poem.

16. What if You Were Mr. Lincoln?

Slavery is evil, and hindsight is easy: of course slavery should have been illegal! But making decisions is never easy. In his book, *You Are the President*, author Nathan Aaseng puts the reader in the White House as the one charged with the responsibility of weighing the evidence and choosing the solution to complex situations. Lincoln's decision to issue the Emancipation Proclamation is one of eight chapters. For each chapter, the author provides a statement of the conflict, possible solutions (and the reasoning behind each of them), the President's choice, and a description of the aftermath of the choice. The four choices facing Lincoln were (1) immediately free all slaves as a matter of principle, (2) leave the issue alone and concentrate on winning the war, (3) gradually phase out slavery with compensation to slave owners, and (4) free only the slaves in the rebelling states as a way to cripple the enemy economically.

Here's one way to use this information: Divide students into groups of four. Each of the four must take one of the four viewpoints noted in the previous paragraph and write a short persuasive speech. Then regroup so that all students with the same opinion are in the same group. They share what they've written and work together on one speech that incorporates the best material from each of the contributors. Each group selects one of its members to participate in a debate. (You could also keep this strictly a writing exercise.)

17. Twenty-eight Days in February

Abraham Lincoln, born February 12, 1809, was very interested in the new art of photography; with 119 images, he was the most photographed person of his time. Choose photographs of Mr. Lincoln to pair with each of February's 28 (or 29) days. Put a different student in charge of each photograph. The student should prepare a short report on what was happening in the country at the time Mr. Lincoln sat for the photo. (If you have less than 28 students, involve some teachers or administrators; if you have more, pair some of the students.)

Post the photographs in a timeline, perhaps down the hallway. Students will notice how much Mr. Lincoln ages during the years of the Civil War. The strong visual impact will underscore the personal toll the responsibility of office had on him.

Here are three good sources for photographs:
     www.abrahamlincolnartgallery.com/archivephoto.htm
     www.physical-lincoln.com/wiki/Abraham_Lincoln_photographs
     www.civil-war.tv/abraham-lincoln-photos.htm

NOTE: Adapt this activity for any time of year, not just during the month of February.

18. Tad Lincoln: The White House Years

President Lincoln's son Tad was eight years old when his father became President and twelve when he left the White House with his mother. By all reports, Tad was a lively child, who constantly interrupted his father and brought all kinds of animals into the house. (The Lincolns were criticized for their parenting style.) Ask students to write Tad's journal for him. *OPTION: they may write a series of letters as Tad, perhaps to a friend back in Springfield.*

19. Re-enact Mr. Lincoln's Life

After students are familiar with Mr. Lincoln's life and have had access to various research tools, divide them into groups of 3-5. Have each group decide on a significant episode in Lincoln's life up to age 21 that influenced his beliefs and his actions as President. Have them prepare a five-minute skit to perform in front of the class.

20. Achievements and Challenges

Instruct students to collect images, documents, quotes, and more about the challenges Mr. Lincoln had to overcome and about what he did during his life that have had an enduring impact on our culture. They may use what they find to create posters or bulletin boards.

> *Challenges*: poverty, no schooling, no family wealth or connections,
> lived far from the centers of power, etc.
> *Achievements*: saving the Union, getting rid of slavery, serving as
> an example of honor and integrity in government and life, etc.

21. Teaching with Historic Places

If you take a trip either to the Lincoln Boyhood National Memorial in Lincoln City, Indiana, or the Lincoln Home in Springfield, Illinois, be sure to check out the excellent "Teaching With Historic Places" lesson plans for grades 5-8 that build on students' experiences at the site. All resources are linked to the site, and students can work at their own pace.

The *Lincoln Boyhood National Memorial (Indiana)* lesson focuses on how Mr. Lincoln's pioneer experience influenced his beliefs, actions, and attitudes as President of the United States. It begins with an "inquiry question" and includes the map of the Lincoln family migration route, four readings about Lincoln's boyhood and his character as President, two illustrations of Lincoln's "sum book" (math) pages, five images of the Lincoln farm in Indiana, and one painting of Lincoln's mother.
Access the lesson at www.nps.gov/nr/twhp/wwwlps/lessons/126libo.

The *Lincoln Home National Historic Site (Illinois)* lesson deals with Lincoln's adult life. It begins with an inquiry question and includes four maps showing where Mr. Lincoln lived, slave and free states in the U.S., and residential election results; four readings about Lincoln in politics, including excerpts from key Lincoln speeches, and newspaper accounts of Lincoln's farewell address and funeral in Springfield; four photographs of the Lincoln home; and one drawing of the Lincoln front parlor.
Access the lesson at www.nps.gov/history/nr/twhp/wwwlps/lessons/127liho.

22. The Lost Art of Writing Letters

Remind students that people in the 19th Century wrote many letters. There were no phones, of course, and people lived some distance from each other; they kept in touch by mail. Have students write letters based on these ideas:

1. It is 1816. You are a neighbor of the Lincoln family in Kentucky. Write a letter to Nancy (Abraham's mother) expressing your thoughts about her two young children.

2. It is 1816. Your name is Caleb Hazel and you're Sarah and Abraham's teacher. Write a letter to their parents about a prank the Lincoln children played in school.

3. It is 1832. You are Abraham Lincoln. You have enlisted in the militia and have been elected captain of your rifle company. For three months you have been involved in the Black Hawk War. Write a letter to your stepmother telling her about your experiences.

4. It is 1838. You live in New Salem and you often gather with other friends at Josiah Speed's General Store to shoot the breeze. You've just met Abraham Lincoln. Write a letter to your mother describing your new friend and the conversations you've had with him.

5. It is 1838. You are a reporter. Write an account of Mr. Lincoln's defense of Henry Truett for the Springfield paper.

6. It is 1841. You are Mary Todd. Write a letter to your sister about Mr. Lincoln. He has just broken your engagement.

7. It is 1845. You live in Springfield and you've just engaged the law firm of Lincoln and Herndon to represent you in a court case. Write a letter to a family member that explains the situation and why you want Mr. Lincoln as your lawyer.

8. It is 1848. You live in Springfield, Illinois, and Abraham Lincoln is your representative in the U.S. Congress. Write a letter to him telling him how you feel about slavery and what you expect him to do.

9. It is 1858. You attend a political debate between Stephen Douglas and Abraham Lincoln, both of whom who are running for U.S. Senate. Write about the debate's effect on you in a letter to a relative who lives far away. Who are you going to vote for?

10. It is 1863. You are Abraham Lincoln, traveling to the battlefield near Gettysburg, Pennsylvania, to dedicate a new military graveyard. Write a letter to your best friend, Joshua Speed, about what you'll say and why.

11. It is 1864. You recently heard Mr. Lincoln deliver his Second Inaugural Address. Write a letter to a friend or relative telling what you think of his remarks.

12. It is 1865. As a resident of Washington, D.C., you hear church bells tolling. Someone says President Lincoln was killed. Write a letter to a friend describing your feelings.

23. Mr. Lincoln in His Own Time

Mr. Lincoln was not admired quite so much in his own time as he is in ours. According to the authors of *An Illustrated Biography* (Philip B. Kunhardt Jr., Philip B. Kunhardt III, Peter W. Kunhardt, and David Herbert Donald), many people regarded him as:

> an "outright buffoon who endangered the nation by his presence. He offended conservatives and radicals alike, so the charges went – not only Southerners, Northern Democrats, and conservative Whigs but anti-slavery forces as well, drawing criticism from all sides. ... He was called a 'Simple Susan,' an 'Illinois beast,' a 'wet rag,' a 'Kentucky mule,' a 'political coward,' a 'butcher,' an 'imbecile,' a 'gorilla,' a 'tyrant.' He was 'weak,' 'timid,' 'foul-tongued,' 'pitiable,' had 'no education,' was 'shallow,' 'dazed,' and 'utterly foolish.'"

At least that's some of what critics of his day reportedly said of him.

Here are the reasons:

- He took forever to make decisions.

- His patience was irritating.

- He paid too much attention to opinions from border states (including Kentucky).

- He changed his mind about slavery. At first he was for preserving slavery and then he issued the Emancipation Proclamation.

- The Emancipation Proclamation didn't really free the slaves, just those in states that had seceded.

- He did a questionable job of fighting the war. He kept firing his generals, and his strategies rarely worked. The military felt that he interfered far too much.

- His Cabinet was full of what some called "misfits" and "thieves."

- He didn't get along with Congress.

- He stepped on some people's civil rights.

- He pardoned the guilty.

- He wasn't "serious" enough. He told too many jokes.

What do students think? Set up debates. You can do this several ways. You might make two-person teams, assigning each team one of the statements above. They can research together, but argue separately. (They won't know who is to argue which side until just before the debate.) Or you can roleplay a person who sees Lincoln more of a buffoon than the savior of the Union and debate with individuals who support him or with the entire class.

24. A Living Travelogue

After studying the places that Lincoln belonged to, invite parents to a "living travelogue" program. For example, have students explore resources such as the Kentucky Lincoln Trail, www.kylincolntrail.com. Each student or group of students can choose one of the 14 stops on the trail and work on some creative way to present the information about each stop on stage (e.g., a skit, a song, a series of movements, artwork, or even the traditional report). *OPTION: Expand and create an original "Lincoln Trail Travelogue," including additional information about places in Kentucky, Indiana, Illinois and Washington, D.C. Videotape the presentation or create a PowerPoint to post on the school website.*

Chapter Four

Where to Find Mr. Lincoln

IN INDIANA

Levi Coffin House
113 U.S. 27 North
Fountain City, IN 47341
www.waynet.org/levicoffin/default.htm

This home of Levi and Catharine Coffin is said to have been a main site for the Underground Railroad during the era leading up to the Emancipation Proclamation. Historians estimate that 2,000 slaves were helped to freedom from this house. The house is open for tours.

Indiana Historical Society
450 West Ohio Street
Indianapolis, IN 46202
www.indianahistory.org

The Indiana Historical Society in downtown Indianapolis features a permanent changing exhibition devoted to the images of Abraham Lincoln, his significance as the 16th President, and his status as an American icon. The Faces of Lincoln exhibition, located on the fourth floor, explores the public perception of Lincoln throughout his life and after his assassination. Visitors can view prints, busts and lithographs of Lincoln as a way to learn more about his political career and his enduring legacy. A smaller version of this exhibit will travel to your school. Contact the museum for more information.

Programs for students. After touring *The Faces of Lincoln* exhibition, students will analyze political cartoons, prints and portraits to observe how Abraham Lincoln's image changed during his lifetime and after his assassination. The program is also available as a distance learning opportunity for students.

Lincoln Boyhood National Memorial
2916 East South Street
P.O. Box 1816
Lincoln, IN 47552
www.nps.gov/libo

The Lincoln Boyhood National Memorial, operated by the National Park Service, preserves the site of the Lincoln family farm, where Abraham Lincoln lived between ages 7 and 21.

Programs for students. The park offers an excellent three-hour tour for students at a cost of $3 per student. The layout of the site and the nature of the tour ensures that students will be entertained and enlightened. A 40-page teacher guide with background information and follow-up activities is available at www.nps.gov/libo/forteachers.

What to see. The outside of the imposing Memorial Visitor's Center is decorated with marble bas relief sculptures presenting five important periods in Mr. Lincoln's life. Inside are a 15-minute movie/orientation and exhibits dealing with the Lincoln family and pioneer life.

The 1820s farm. A short walk from the Memorial Visitor's Center is a recreated 1820s farm, similar to that on which Lincoln lived as a youth. (April-September it operates as a living-history farm.) Members of the farm family, in period dress, work the farm much as they would have in 1820, chopping wood, splitting rails, cooking over an open fire, shearing sheep and carding wool, making soap, cultivating the garden and smoking hams. Nearby fields are cultivated using early 19th Century methods. Students will see the site of the original cabin and its split rail fences. A guide will greet students and tell them about the farm's activities, but the emphasis is on giving them time to explore and ask questions on their own.

The walking tour. There are two routes from the memorial building to the farm. The shorter route passes by the small cemetery where Lincoln's mother, Nancy Hanks Lincoln, is buried. The other, which takes a half hour to hike, is called the "Trail of the Twelve Stones." The wide, well-tended pathway meanders through the woods; stops along the way feature stones taken from buildings connected with important times in Lincoln's life (e.g., a stone from the field at Gettysburg; a stone from the Old Soldier's Home at which he wrote the Emancipation Proclamation). Plaques explain the origin and significance of each stone.

The Lincoln Pioneer Village and Museum
End of Main Street
Rockport, IN
www.lincolnpioneervillage.org

The Lincoln Pioneer Village consists of 14 log cabins showcasing artifacts similar to what Mr. Lincoln would have encountered in the years he spent in Spencer County, Indiana (1816-1830), including a hutch built by his father and a dress worn by his sister.

Lincoln State Park
Highway 162, Box 316
Lincoln City, IN 47552
www.in.gov/dnr/parklake/2979.htm

The 1,747 acre park was established in 1932 as a memorial to Nancy Hanks. Much of the park looks as it did when Abraham Lincoln's family settled nearby (when he was seven years old). The grave of his sister, Sarah Lincoln Grisby, is here, as is the restored home of Colonel Jones, Abraham Lincoln's first employer. There are plans for the Lincoln amphitheatre to featured plays such as *Young Mr. Lincoln* during the bicentennial year of his birth and, possibly, beyond.

IN KENTUCKY

The Kentucky Abraham Lincoln Bicentennial Commission organized several sites in Kentucky with connections to Mr. Lincoln into the "Lincoln Heritage Trail." Twenty-seven new historical markers tell the history of each site and its significance in Mr. Lincoln's life and career. The website www.kylincolntrail.com includes an interactive map. Click around to find a photo, a description of both the site and the locale, and links to stories about Mr. Lincoln that involve the site. Here are some places directly connected to Mr. Lincoln and his era:

Abraham Lincoln Birthplace National Historic Site
2995 Lincoln Farm Road
Hodgenville, KY 42748
www.nps.gov/abli

Thomas and Nancy Lincoln settled on the 348-acre Sinking Spring Farm near Hodgenville in 1808. Two months later, on Feb. 12, 1809, Abraham Lincoln was born. On July 17, 1916, Congress established this memorial as a national park.

Programs for students. The birthplace is enshrined within a neo-classical memorial building. There are 56 steps up to the imposing memorial, one for each year of Mr. Lincoln's life. A video and interactive exhibits in the Visitor's Center cover Mr. Lincoln's experiences throughout his life. *Contact the site for information on school tours.*

Abraham Lincoln Boyhood Home
U.S. 31 E
Hodgenville, KY 42748
www.nps.gov/abli/knob-creek-farm-cabin-restoration.htm

Abraham Lincoln was two when his family moved to Knob Creek, several miles from his birthplace and on the main route from Louisville to Nashville. There are plans to develop the site, but right now it mainly consists of a replica cabin, similar to the one Mr. Lincoln lived in from 1811-1816. He said in later years that the first home he could remember was "the Knob Creek place" and that he remembered it very well.

Abraham Lincoln Library and Museum
6965 Cumberland Gap Parkway
Harrogate, TN 37752
www.lmunet.edu/museum/civilwarcamp/index.html

Located at Cumberland Gap, less than five miles from Middlesboro, Kentucky, the museum displays artifacts and imagery related both to Lincoln and the Civil War.

Programs for students. Teachers can arrange visits for school groups. The website offers activities and information for study (e.g., "Children In The Civil War" artifact-based activities, games, home remedies, Underground Railroad codes, letter writing, and printable issues of *Soldier's Yearly*, the Lincoln Letters for Kids "newsletter" of events from the 1860s).

Ashland - The Henry Clay Estate

120 Sycamore Road
Lexington, KY 40502
www.henryclay.org

Senator Henry Clay, Lincoln's political mentor and hero, built his home on this site. After his death in 1852, Clay's heirs sold the land to his son, James Brown Clay, who built the current house in 1857. It is on the National Register of Historic Places.

Programs for students. Ashland offers a tour for grades 2-5 which emphasizes what a child's life was like in the 1800s and a tour for grades 6-12 that emphasizes Henry Clay's importance in American history. Both tours include a video, plus a walk through the grounds, outbuildings and mansion.

Camp Nelson Civil War Heritage Park and National Cemetery

6614 Danville Pike
Nicholasville, KY 40356
www.campnelson.org

During the Civil War, Camp Nelson was the largest African American recruitment camp in Kentucky and the third-largest in the nation. Many of the 5,400 black recruits, who were emancipated upon enlistment, brought their families with them to Camp Nelson in the hope that they also would be freed. There is an impressive visitor's center, still under development. Designated a U.S. cemetery for Union dead in 1867, it remains a military cemetery. *Call for information on curriculum-based education programs.*

Columbus-Belmont State Park

350 Park Road
Columbus, KY 42032
http://parks.ky.gov/findparks/recparks/cb

Called the "Gibralter of the West," Columbus-Belmont State Park on Kentucky's western border played a fascinating role in the Civil War. This site of fortifications built by the Confederates was later occupied by Union forces. It was the scene of Gen. Ulysses S. Grant's first active engagement in the Civil War. Some of the artillery, which shelled Union troops, and the six-ton anchor that held a great chain stretching across the Mississippi River to block Union gunboat traffic are displayed. A farmhouse that served as a hospital during the war remains (it is now the park museum).

Programs for students. On a 2.5-mile self-guided hiking trail, dramatic images of the Civil War come to mind when walking the bluffs and massive earthenworks that formed Confederate trenches. Students can learn about the area and the Civil War in the renovated museum. Annual "Civil War Days" each October includes an "education day" with special activities for students. Get a teacher packet at http://parks.ky.gov/findparks/recparks/cb/groups.

Farmington Historic Plantation
3033 Bardstown Road
Louisville, KY 40205
www.historichomes.org/farmington

Farmington, a 14-room Federal-style home, was the boyhood home of Joshua Speed, Mr. Lincoln's close friend. Although interpretation focuses on the 1830s when the Speed family operated a hemp plantation there, there is also emphasis on the Speeds' ties to Mr. Lincoln.

Programs for students. Instead of a video introduction, Farmington boasts a newly installed sound and light program which focuses on the museum's objects and artifacts. Students sit in semi-darkness in the center of a room and listen to voices with music and sound effects that recount the history and significance of the site.

The home and outbuildings tour is tailored to age and grade levels; its focus is on differences between daily life in the early 19th Century and the early 21st Century. In addition, Farmington offers two educational programs that connect directly with Mr. Lincoln:

1. The two-hour "Detective for a Day" program includes a tour of the historic house and grounds followed by a session introducing students to research using primary sources relating to Mr. Lincoln, slavery and the Speed family. In small groups, students study documents and artifacts, respond to questions, and report findings to the whole group.

2. The one-hour "Lincoln Logs" program for younger students includes a tour of the site, on-site writing activities, and activities for the teacher to conduct back in the classroom.

Teachers can download a packet that includes basic information on Farmington, a vocabulary list, a timeline relating events at Farmington to significant events of the period, and a lesson plan for a pre-visit activity for classes involved in the "Detective for a Day" program.

Hardin County Museum
201 W. Dixie Avenue
Elizabethtown, KY 42701
www.hardinkyhistory.org

Focuses on the story of Hardin County from early Indian inhabitants to modern times. "Abraham Lincoln Family and Friends" exhibit is a collection of 12 informative markers.

Helm Cemetery
U.S. 31 W and Ky. Hwy. 447
Elizabethtown, KY

This pioneer cemetery includes the graves of John LaRue Helm, who served two incomplete terms as governor of Kentucky, and his son, Confederate Gen. Ben Hardin Helm, who died at the Battle of Chickamauga on Sept. 20, 1863. General Helm and Lincoln married half-sisters, Emilie Todd and Mary Todd, the daughters of Robert S. Todd of Lexington.

Jefferson Davis State Historic Site
Highway 68E
Fairview, KY 42221
www.parks.ky.gov/findparks/histparks/jd

The Jefferson Davis State Historic Site, featuring the tallest poured-in-place concrete obelisk in the world, is a memorial to the President of the Confederacy, Lincoln's fellow Kentucky native (born just 8 months and 100 miles apart) and political adversary during the Civil War.

Kentucky Historical Society
100 W. Broadway
Frankfort, KY 40601
www.history.ky.gov

The Kentucky Historical Society's new Lincoln exhibit is in the Thomas D. Clark Center for Kentucky History. Through images and artifacts, including his pocket watch, the Society presents the personal side of Lincoln and his Kentucky relationships. The library and special collections include documents and family-history resources that connect Lincoln's genealogy and other Kentucky families. The Historical Society sponsors the HistoryMobile, the National History Day competition, the Junior Historical Society, and the History Zone.

Programs for students. As well as touring the exhibit, students will meet costumed interpreters who roleplay individuals, such as Mary Todd, affected by Lincoln's presidency. Curriculum materials that relate to the exhibit are in continual development. Teachers can download a general guide to field trips and other information and resources from the museum's website. From www.history.ky.gov, click "Programs" and find a *For Schools* list with "Field Trips" link.

Lincoln Heritage House
140 Freeman Lake Park Road
Elizabethtown, KY 42701
www.touretown.com/lincolnheritagehouse.shtml

This pioneer home of the Hardin-Thomas family was built about 1789. Thomas Lincoln, father of Abraham, did carpentry and cabinet work on the four-room log house. Thomas Lincoln lived in Hardin County for several years. *Open June to October.*

Lincoln Homestead State Park
5079 Lincoln Park Road
Springfield, KY 40069
http://parks.ky.gov/findparks/recparks/lh

The original home of Mr. Lincoln's mother, Nancy Hanks, is in this park. There are also replicas of the 1782 cabin and blacksmith shop where Lincoln's father was raised and learned his trade, plus the home of Mordecai Lincoln, Abraham Lincoln's uncle. The site showcases reproductions of traditional pioneer split-rail fence and pioneer furniture. *Open May through September.*

Lincoln Marriage Temple
Old Fort Harrod State Park
100 South College Street
Harrodsburg, KY 40330
http://parks.ky.gov/findparks/recparks/fh

The Lincoln Marriage Cabin stands inside the "temple," a red brick building in the shape of a cross built in 1911. The cabin was moved from its original site in the Beech Fork Settlement, where Thomas and Nancy Hanks Lincoln married, to the Old Fort Harrod State Park. *Open February through March.*

The Lincoln Museum and Lincoln Statue
66 Lincoln Square
Hodgenville, KY 42748
www.lincolnmuseum-ky.org

This museum in Hodgenville's historic central square includes twelve dioramas showing pivotal times in Lincoln's life. Other exhibits include rare newspaper clippings, campaign posters, and Lincoln memorabilia. An art gallery on the second floor features paintings, drawings and other artworks portraying Lincoln.

Special Programs. The museum participates in LaRue County's annual "Lincoln Days" celebration, scheduled the first weekend in October (details at www.lincolndays.org).

Mary Todd Lincoln House
578 West Main Street
Lexington, KY 40507
www.mtlhouse.org

The Todd family moved to this two-story Georgian-style house in 1832, when Mary was 13. After their marriage, Mary Todd and Abraham Lincoln visited here frequently.

Mordecai Lincoln House
859-336-7461
Springfield, KY
http://parks.ky.gov/findparks/recparks/lh

This is the home of Mordecai Lincoln, eldest son of Captain Abraham Lincoln (the President's grandfather) and his wife Bersheba. Mordecai was President Lincoln's favorite uncle. This two-story house is located on its original site. Mordecai Lincoln was a leading citizen of Washington County. The home is available for tours.

Perryville Battlefield State Historic Site
1825 Battlefield Road
Perryville, KY 40468
www.parks.ky.gov/findparks/histparks/pb

The Perryville site commemorates the battle on October 8, 1862, the only Civil War battle of any size in central Kentucky. Over 7,600 soldiers were dead, injured, or missing in the South's last serious attempt to gain possession of Kentucky. The battlefield itself is one of the least-altered Civil War sites in the nation; vistas are virtually those that soldiers saw in 1862.

Programs for students. The site includes the museum, the battlefield itself, and various monuments. Costumed interpreters are on hand to explain the battle and its significance to visiting students. Past participants rave about the four-hour "School of the Soldier" program in which elementary students role-play the lives of soldiers in 1862.

Special programs. An annual commemoration of the battle takes place each year. Visitors can see a reenactment of the battle, visit the tents, and chat with re-enactors and various sutlers (storekeepers).

Sarah Bush Johnston Lincoln Memorial
Freeman Lake Park
140 Freeman Lake Park Road
Elizabethtown, KY 42701
www.touretown.com/sarahbush.shtml

This memorial cabin honoring Sarah Bush Johnston Lincoln, who became Lincoln's stepmother when he was ten, was built in 1992 from 122-year-old hand-hewn logs. It is similar to the cabin Sarah lived in when she married Thomas Lincoln. *Open weekends during summer; other times by appointment.*

White Hall State Historic Site
500 White Hall Shrine Road
Richmond, KY 40475
www.parks.ky.gov/findparks/histparks/wh

This is the home of Cassius Marcellus Clay, emancipationist, newspaper publisher, and friend to Lincoln. Lincoln appointed Clay as minister to Russia. Clay's restored 44-room Italianate mansion was built in 1799 and was remodeled in the 1860s. In addition to the heirloom and period furnishings, White Hall has many features that were unique for its day, including indoor running water and central heating.

IN ILLINOIS

Lincoln Home National Historic Site
413 South Eighth Street
Springfield, IL 62701

This is the only home owned by Abraham and Mary Todd Lincoln. If you can't make a field trip, your class can take a room-by-room virtual tour of the house online at www.nps.gov/history/museum/exhibits/liho.

Oak Ridge Cemetery
1500 Monument Ave.
Springfield, IL 62702

The public receiving vault was the site of Lincoln's funeral. The Lincoln Tomb is the final resting place of Abraham Lincoln, his wife Mary, and three of their four sons, Edward, William and Thomas. (The eldest, Robert T. Lincoln, is buried in Arlington National Cemetery.)

ELSEWHERE

Lincoln Memorial
West Potomac Park, National Mall
Washington, DC
www.nps.gov/linc

Perhaps the most famous Lincoln site, this massive memorial in the nation's capitol contains the well-known seated statue of the Great Emancipator enshrined within columns at the building's entrance. Learn about the Lincoln Memorial from anywhere, 24 hours a day, by listening to any of 13 brief Ranger Talks via phone: 202-747-3420.

Lincoln's Pennsylvania Ancestors
Lancaster and Berks Counties, PA
www.palincoln.org/lincoln_in_pa/ancestry_in_pa

Ancestors of President Lincoln migrated from Massachusetts and New Jersey to settle in Pennsylvania for a few years before moving into Virginia and on to the western frontier. This website traces the Pennsylvania Lincolns who were the 16th President's forebears.

Lincoln's Virginia Ancestors
Rockingham County
Linville, VA
www.hmdb.org/Marker.asp?Marker=15634

An historical marker stands at the Lincoln house (built about 1800 by Captain Jacob Lincoln, the President's great-uncle), which is near the original 1768 Lincoln homestead. Markers for five generations of Lincolns and two family slaves are in the cemetery on the hill.

Chapter Five

Resources for Learning About Mr. Lincoln

1. BOOKS

Thousands of books about Abraham Lincoln, the Civil War, and slavery are available for young readers. This list includes some of the more recently published books that have proven especially popular with middle school students.

Non-fiction about Mr. Lincoln

Armstrong, Jennifer – *A Three-Minute Speech: Lincoln's Remarks at Gettysburg*

> This account of the significance of the Gettysburg Address begins with the Declaration of Independence and explains the young republic's struggle with slavery. It also discusses Lincoln's political ideas and his rise in politics. The exact text of the Gettysburg Address is included, with an analysis of why it had such an effect on Americans both then and now.

Bial, Raymond – *Where Lincoln Walked*

> This photo-essay includes a brief biography of President Lincoln, a list of locations where he walked, and photographs of places, buildings and objects significant in his life. Includes a map and a list of places to visit.

Bishop, Jim – *The Day Lincoln Was Shot*

> In this hour-by-hour "history-as-mystery," the author leads readers through the lives of all the players in the assassination drama. This is an old book, but as a gripping read for both adolescents and adults, it stands the test of time ... just like Mr. Lincoln himself. Having been reissued in paperback a couple of times since the hardback debuted, you can still buy it and libraries still have it. Best for older students and teachers.

Burgan, Michael – *The Gettysburg Address*

> Details the events that led to the Battle of Gettysburg, including an overview of slavery, the Civil War and Lincoln's election and presidency.

Davis, Kenneth C. *Don't Know Much About Abraham Lincoln.*

> The narrative in this biography consists of a series of questions and answers. Includes informational sidebars, maps and historic photos.

Elliot, Ron – *Through the Eyes of Lincoln: A Modern Photographic Journey*
(Photos by John W. Snell)

> Large, beautiful photographs of places important to Mr. Lincoln dominate this coffee-table book. The text takes readers from the Lincoln birthplace in Kentucky, through Indiana and Illinois, to Washington, and back to Lincoln's grave in Springfield. It also includes some historic photographs and maps.

Freedman, Russell – *Lincoln: A Photobiography*

Winner of awards, including the Newbery Medal, it has been described as "the most complete and enjoyable children's book ever written about one of the nation's most fascinating and important figures." Copiously illustrated with period photographs and drawings.

Giblin, James Cross – *Good Brother, Bad Brother: The Story of Edwin Booth & John Wilkes Booth*

Fascinating dual biography compares John Wilkes Booth to his older brother, Edwin, who was considered the finest classical actor of his time. He also supported the North, whereas John Wilkes harbored a passionate dislike of the North and especially of Abraham Lincoln. Best for older students.

Hale, Sarah Elder, ed. – *Abraham Lincoln: Defender of the Union*

The 13 articles in this anthology cover Lincoln's family, causes of the war, the Lincoln-Douglas Debates, the assassination and more. Numerous illustrations, sidebars, maps and historic photographs make for very interesting reading. Most of the information appeared first in *Cobblestone* and *Appleseeds* magazines.

Harness, Cheryl – *Young Abe Lincoln: The Frontier Days, 1809-1837*

Explores the early life of Abraham Lincoln, emphasizing his efforts to educate himself.

Herbert, Janis – *Abraham Lincoln for Kids*

This biography of Lincoln combines a well-written narrative with an assessment of the effects of his decisions as President. Activities include "Draw a Political Cartoon," "Learn Morse Code," and more. Includes historical photos and illustrations, a timeline, list of places to visit, and an annotated bibliography.

Holzer, Harold, ed. – *Abraham Lincoln, The Writer: A Treasury of His Greatest Speeches and Letters*

Abraham Lincoln tells his own story, beginning with the words scribbled in the margin of his arithmetic book; the collection includes poems, letters, excerpts from speeches and debates, his inaugural addresses, telegrams, notes on the law, and more. Each piece of writing is accompanied by an informative introduction explaining its context and significance. Best for older students.

Holzer, Harold – *The President Is Shot! The Assassination of Abraham Lincoln*

Beginning on the day Lincoln died and moving backwards in time, this account shows why Lincoln was both admired and despised by his contemporaries. Includes historic photos and illustrations. Best for older students.

Leidner, Gordon – *Abraham Lincoln: The Complete Book of Facts, Quizzes, and Trivia*

For information junkies. Set up your own Jeopardy or Quick Recall game using the information and questions in this book.

Marrin, Albert – *Commander In Chief: Abraham Lincoln and the Civil War*

Excellent biography on Lincoln as war leader. The author puts his subject in context, with plenty of information about 19th Century life and politics. Best for older students.

Meltzer, Milton – *Lincoln In His Own Words*

Excerpts from Abraham Lincoln's speeches, letters and other writings tell the story of his life and the development of his ideas. Best for older students.

Morris, Jeffrey – *The Lincoln Way*

Focuses on the development of Abraham Lincoln's ideas and how he made his most important decisions, including preserving the Union and freeing the slaves.

Murphy, Jim – *The Long Road to Gettysburg*

By telling the story of the Battle of Gettysburg through the journeys of two young soldiers, the author conveys the boredom, excitement and terror of the battle. Powerful photos show the kind of historic detail that's often missing in books for adolescents. An epilogue explains what happened to the two soldiers after the battle. Best for older students.

Pinkney, Andrea Davis – *Abraham Lincoln: Letters from a Slave Girl*

Fictional correspondence between President Abraham Lincoln and a twelve-year-old slave girl reveals Lincoln's views about slavery, the progress of the war, and his decision to issue the Emancipation Proclamation in 1863. Best for older students.

Rabin, Staton – *Mr. Lincoln's Boys*

According to all accounts, Tad and Willie Lincoln, who were children when Mr. Lincoln came to the White House, were rambunctious, noisy and full of fun. Great illustrations. Best for younger children.

Roop, Connie – *Grace's Letter to Lincoln*

A fictional version of a true story: the girl who recommended that Lincoln grow a beard to win more votes. The real letter and Lincoln's reply are included.

Sandburg, Carl – *Abe Lincoln Grows Up*

First published in 1926 and never out of print, Carl Sandburg's two-volume biography of Lincoln still lives for people of all ages. *Abe Lincoln Grows Up* consists of the first 27 chapters of the original work, covering the years in Kentucky and Indiana. Carl Sandburg's poetic language and rhythms make this an excellent choice for reading aloud.

Stone, Tanya – *Abraham Lincoln: A Photographic Story of a Life*

Lots of photos of people and places enliven this biography. Emphasis is on how a struggling

small town lawyer became President and one of America's most revered leaders.
Sullivan, George – *Picturing Lincoln: Famous Photographs That Popularized the President*

The author examines five photographs of Lincoln, describing how they have been used throughout history. Best for older students.

Books about Slavery

Armentrout, David and Patricia – *The Emancipation Proclamation*

Puts the Emancipation Proclamation in context, with information about slavery and the causes of the Civil War.

Hopkinson, Deborah – *Sweet Clara and the Freedom Quilt*

Young Clara, a slave, sews a quilt that becomes a map depicting the route of the Underground Railroad and the way north to freedom. Best for grades K-3.

Hamilton, Virginia – *Many Thousand Gone: African Americans from Slavery to Freedom.*
(Illustrated by Leo and Diane Dillon)

This book offers 34 brief vignettes of slavery in America from its beginning to the end of the Civil War. Best for grades 6-8.

Lester, Julius – *Day of Tears: A Novel in Dialogue*

This fictionalized account of the biggest slave auction in American history, which took place in Savannah, Georgia, in 1859, uses dialogue from multiple points of view to bring the events of that day to life for young readers. This book was the winner of the 2006 Coretta Scott King Author Award. Best for grades 6-8.

McComb, Marianne – *The Emancipation Proclamation*

This book describes in very straightforward and accurate text the roots of slavery in the United States, why some people and states were for it and others were opposed to it, why President Lincoln issued the Proclamation when he did, who the Proclamation freed and who it did not, and some of the effects it had on future events. Best for grades 6-8.

McKissack, Patricia C., & Fredrick L. McKissack – *Days of Jubilee: The End of Slavery in the United States*

Slaves' personal accounts chronicle the various days that led up to the Emancipation Proclamation, the 13th Amendment and the eventual freedom of all slaves. This book is a 2004 Coretta Scott King Author Honor Book.

Books about the Civil War

Armstrong, Jennifer – *Photo by Brady: A Picture of the Civil War*

> Photographs from over a century ago bring the people and events of the Civil War to life. These striking historical images are the work of Matthew Brady, a pioneer in the art of photography.

Clinton, Catherine – *Hold the Flag High*

> This picture book tells the story of Sergeant William H. Carney, the first African-American to be awarded the Congressional Medal of Honor. A sergeant in the Massachusetts 54th, he saved the flag from hitting the ground during the assault on Fort Carney, an incident famously depicted in the movie *Glory*. The pictures do not glamorize the story, nor are they excessively violent. Nevertheless, the book is best for older students, not the usual picture book audience, and will have an emotional impact on everyone, including adults.

Damon, Duane – *Growing Up in the Civil War*

> Describes what life was like for young people during the Civil War, including those who were slaves and those who were soldiers. Lots of photographs.

Fleischman, Paul – *Bull Run*

> The story of the Civil War's first battle is told by sixteen alternating characters. Excellent insight into the causes, conduct, and effects of the war. Winner of the Scott O'Dell Historical Fiction Award. Best for third grade and up.

Herbert, Janis – *The Civil War for Kids: A History with 21 Activities*

> This comprehensive book offers hands-on activities and readable information about the Civil War from the secession debates to Appomattox. Best for third grade and up.

Murphy, Jim – *The Boys' War: Confederate and Union Soldiers Talk About the Civil War*

> Hundreds of boys ages 16 and younger served in both the Confederate and Union armies as drummers, buglers, telegraphers and soldiers. The author relies on selections from their letters, diaries and memoirs to tell their stories, including why they chose to fight, their experiences in camp and in battle and, for those who survived, what happened to them after the war. Best for third grade and up.

Sandler, Martin – *The Civil War*

> The story of the Civil War told through primary sources, including illustrations and photographs, songs, letters, journals, poems and speeches.

Wisler, G. Clifton – *When Johnny Went Marching: Young Americans Fight the Civil War*

> Thousands of boys under the age of 16, some as young as 10, participated in the Civil War as drummers, drivers, hospital orderlies, telegraphers and soldiers. Each young person's story is told in two or three pages.

Fiction featuring Mr. Lincoln as a character

Deutsch, Stacia, & Rhody Cohon – *Lincoln's Legacy*

> What if Abraham Lincoln never freed the slaves? That's the question Abigail's history teacher asks her. Then he recruits Abigail and her friends to go back in time so that they can convince President Lincoln not to give up. Best for younger students.

McMullan, Margaret – *How I Found the Strong: A Civil War Story*

> A boy left behind when his father and brother go off to fight for the South in the Civil War has experiences that change his mind about slavery, courage and the reasons for war. This coming of age story is based on a family manuscript. Includes many details about life in Civil War Mississippi. Best for older students.

Pearsall, Shelley – *Trouble Don't Last*

> In this historical adventure story, two slaves escape from Kentucky and head for Canada via the Underground Railroad. This book is the winner of the 2003 Scott O'Dell Historical Fiction Award.

Wisler, G. Clifton – *Mr. Lincoln's Drummer*

> This engaging historical novel recounts the adventures of Willie Johnson, a Civil War drummer, who became the youngest recipient of the Congressional Medal of Honor.

Myers, Anna – *Assassin*

> Told from the viewpoint of John Wilkes Booth as well from the perspective of a fictional young girl, this novel details Booth's plot against the President. Best for older students.

2. SCREEN (TV, FILM, DVD, VHS, WEB VIDEO)

Here are some of the more educational and entertaining recent videos and DVDs about Abraham Lincoln that are suitable for intermediate and middle school classrooms:

Abraham and Mary Lincoln: A House Divided
PBS American Experience, DVD, 2001, 360 minutes

> A dual biography from the PBS television series. Explores the couple's different childhoods, their marriage and their years in the White House.

Abraham Lincoln: Preserving the Union
A&E Biography, DVD, 1997,100 minutes

> Tells the life of Lincoln from his home in Illinois to his assassination.

The Assassination of Abraham Lincoln
PBS American Experience, DVD, 2009, 90 minutes
View it online: www.pbs.org/wgbh/americanexperience/assassination

> Narration and interviews with the nation's foremost Lincoln scholars recount a great American drama: two tumultuous months when the joy of peace was shattered by the heartache of the President's death.

The Civil War
PBS series by Emmy-winning director Ken Burns, 5 DVD set, 1990, 690 minutes

> Superb quintessential documentary on the Civil War.

Interview with Abraham Lincoln
DVD, 2005, 30 minutes

> Order this enactment of a hypothetical interview from Library Video website, www.libraryvideo.com/servlet/viajero/product/V8192. (Teaching guide included.)

I, Too, Am a Kentuckian

> This program is an extended edition of "Kentucky Life," a Kentucky Educational Television series. Details at KET website: www.ket.org/kentuckylife/1400s/kylife1427.html.

Kentucky's Underground Railroad – Passage To Freedom

> This KET program can be viewed online: www.ket.org/underground/resources/segments01.htm

Life of Lincoln Interactive
Indiana Historical Society, DVD, 2004, 50 minutes

> Abraham Lincoln's life from his early days to his assassination. Activities include interpreting primary sources, analyzing Lincoln speeches and other research projects. Three-disc set includes video, interactive DVD and 79-page downloadable teacher guide.

Lincoln's New Salem: Turning Point
  View it online: www.lincolnsnewsalem.com

> This is the same excellent 20-minute video shown at the Visitor's Center at New Salem, Indiana, a reconstruction of the town Lincoln lived in as a young man.

Lincoln
  History Channel, DVD, 2006, 140 minutes

> The History Channel takes an in-depth look at the personal life of the Great Emancipator, using dramatic reenactments and interviews with leading Lincoln biographers. Told from the perspective of the President himself.

Lincoln: Man or Myth
  History Channel, VHS, 2005, 50 minutes

> An exploration of the life and legacy of Abraham Lincoln.

Looking for Lincoln
  Produced by Kunhardt McGee Productions & Inkwell Films, DVD, 2009, 120 minutes
  View it online: www.pbs.org/wnet/lookingforlincoln/video/watch-looking-for-lincoln/290

> Historian Henry Louis Gates Jr.'s quest to piece together Lincoln's complex life takes him from Illinois to Gettysburg to Washington, D.C., and face-to-face with people who live with Lincoln every day – relic hunters, re-enactors and others for whom the study of Lincoln is a passion. Historians, living Presidents, educators and Lincoln scholars contribute commentary. Get more video and interactives at: www.pbs.org/wnet/lookingforlincoln.

Mr. Lincoln's Springfield
  National Heritage series from Finley-Holiday Films, VHS, 1998, 30 minutes

> Historic photographs and reminiscences describe Abraham Lincoln's life in Springfield, Illinois, including information about his family.

Ordinary People, Extraordinary Courage: Men and Women of the Underground Railroad in the Indiana and Kentucky Borderland

> This DVD can be borrowed for classroom use from the permanent exhibit housed at the Carnegie Center for Art & History in New Albany, Indiana.
> www.carnegiecenter.org/exhibit_undergroundRR.html

Well Done, Indiana
  Indiana Historical Society, DVD, 2006, 30 minutes

> An engaging Civil War documentary featuring interviews, first-person accounts, and rare historical photographs and archival materials.

Young Abe Lincoln
  Indiana Historical Society, DVD, 2004, 27 minutes

> A documentary about Abraham Lincoln's Indiana years. Explores the influences southern Indiana made on Lincoln's character.

3. INTERNET SITES

There are literally thousands of sites devoted to Mr. Lincoln on the Internet. Here are some of the better ones.

FOR STUDENTS & TEACHERS ...

Abraham Lincoln
The History Channel
www.history.com/presidents/Lincoln

> Nicely designed site is easy for students to explore. Links include a biography, timeline, image gallery, video gallery, important speeches and quizzes. A few short commercials don't get in the way.

Abraham Lincoln Bicentennial
www.lincolnbicentennial.gov

> The interactive timeline, virtual tour of significant places in Lincoln's life, and the quiz-question-of-the-day will capture students' attention quickly. The site includes a calendar listing of Lincoln-related events.

Abraham Lincoln Biography
The Lincoln Home
www.nps.gov/liho/forteachers/upload/Lincoln%20MS%20Biography.pdf

> Excellent online biography for grades 5-8. Includes comprehension questions and vocabulary lists. Very few photos and images, however.

The Abraham Lincoln Presidential Library
www.alincoln-library.com

> Nicely designed site includes articles on Mr. Lincoln's achievements, his family, favorite jokes and quotes, the Lincoln Museum, the Lincoln penny and the Lincoln library.

Abraham Lincoln Presidential Library and Museum
Timeline
www.alplm.org/timeline/timeline.html

> This excellent and very well-designed timeline will take students through Mr. Lincoln's life year by year.

Abraham Lincoln – Encarta Online
http://encarta.msn.com/encyclopedia_761577113/Abraham_Lincoln.html

> This lengthy article covers every period of Lincoln's life and career. A few images and an audio file of a reading of the Gettysburg Address are included.

Eyewitness to History: Mr. Lincoln

This award-winning website (with a few annoying ads you soon learn to ignore) presents history through the perspective of those who lived it. Five accounts deal with Mr. Lincoln. Each account is preceded by a summary of the importance of the event.

- View of President Lincoln, 1861
  Ordinary citizens' opinions of the 16th President
  www.eyewitnesstohistory.com/lincoln2.htm
- President Lincoln Signs the Emancipation Proclamation, 1863
  Mr. Lincoln and his groundbreaking document that freed the Southern slaves
  www.eyewitnesstohistory.com/emancipation.htm
- Lincoln's Gettysburg Address, 1863
  A report by John Hay, Mr. Lincoln's private secretary
  www.eyewitnesstohistory.com/gtsburgaddress.htm
- President Lincoln enters Richmond, 1865
  Abraham Lincoln tours the capital of the Confederacy after its capture
  www.eyewitnesstohistory.com/richmond.htm
- The Death of President Lincoln, 1865
  What happened after President Lincoln was shot at Ford's Theater
  www.eyewitnesstohistory.com/lincoln.htm

The History Place Presents A. Lincoln
www.historyplace.com/lincoln

This site contains a detailed timeline of Mr. Lincoln's life, with speeches and photographs embedded. The site also offers a timeline for the Civil War.

A House Divided: America in the Age of Lincoln
The Digital History Project
www.digitalhistory.uh.edu/ahd/exhibit_menu.html

The Digital History Project is an interactive, multimedia history of the U.S. from the Revolution to the present – an online textbook. A subsite, "The House Divided," presents the story of Lincoln, his times, and the Civil War in well-organized soundbites, each with illustrations or video. Great site for students as an introduction to the era. For teachers, there are classroom handouts, learning modules, lesson plans and resource guides.

Kentucky's Lincoln Heritage Trail
www.kylincolntrail.com

This site, a cooperative effort by the Kentucky Heritage Council, the Kentucky Department of Tourism, and the Kentucky Transportation Cabinet, begins with an interactive map of all Lincoln-related sites in Kentucky that welcome student visits. If students click on the site, they're taken to a pop-up that explains its significance, tells a story from Lincoln's life, and offers additional information about the history or the time period. You can access the 27 stories directly at www.kylincolntrail.com/lincolnStory.aspx. These stories are useful for research on Mr. Lincoln's Kentucky connections.

The Lincoln Institute
www.abrahamlincoln.org

With private funding, the Lincoln Institute concentrates on providing all kinds of information for Lincoln scholars, from kids to seniors. It runs several other sites with specific content, and it keeps Mr. Lincoln's myspace page up-to-date.

Abraham Lincoln's Classroom – www.abrahamlincolnsclassroom.org
Mr. Lincoln's White House – www.mrlincolnswhitehouse.org
Mr. Lincoln & Friends – www.mrlincolnandfriends.org
Mr. Lincoln and the Founders – www.mrlincolnandthefounders.org
Mr. Lincoln and Freedom – www.mrlincolnandfreedom.org
Abraham Lincoln on MySpace – www.myspace.com/lincolninstitute

Lincoln's Kentucky
The Filson Historical Society
www.filsonhistorical.org/lincoln

Well-designed, succinct overview of Mr. Lincoln's life and legacy. Great for student research.

The Lincoln Log
www.thelincolnlog.org

Pick a day, any day, in Lincoln's life and enter into this site's search box to find out exactly what Abraham Lincoln was doing on that day.

Lincoln Quiz - Lincoln Bicentennial Commission
www.lincolnbicentennial.gov/for-kids/honest-abe-quiz

Young children will enjoy the 16-question quiz at this site.

Spartacus Educational
www.spartacus.schoolnet.co.uk/USAlincoln.htm

This eclectic British website has a very nice interactive biography of President Lincoln. Good for student research.

PRIMARILY FOR TEACHERS ...

Abraham Lincoln Online
www.abrahamlincolnonline.com (click on *RESOURCES*)

Guide to learning about Lincoln via the net. Includes links to images, speeches, articles, field trip sites, museums, historical sites and much more Lincoln-related info on the Internet.

The Illinois Hitorical Digitization Project
http://dig.lib.niu.edu

> The Illinois Historical Digitization Project at Northern Illinois University Libraries provides multiple websites which offer primary documents, interpretive materials, and multi-format resources (images, video, maps, song recordings) related to United States and Illinois history from 1818-1896. Lesson plans utilize portions of the primary documents available on the sites, as well as sources from other reputable history websites such as the Library of Congress's American Memory site. The Teaching Future Historians site (http://dig.lib.niu.edu/teachers/index.html) compiles all the lesson plans in one easy-to-access website, where teachers can print the lesson plans and necessary readings for course use.

ISBA Resources for Teachers
The Illinois State Bar Association
www.illinoisbar.org/teachers/lincoln/links.html

> A very complete collection of high quality Lincoln links. Useful to teachers in Illinois and everywhere else. Includes links to places, documents, Lincoln's tomb and much more.

Kentucky Abraham Lincoln Bicentennial Commission
www.kylincoln.org

> The Kentucky Abraham Lincoln Bicentennial Commission focuses on Lincoln's connections to Kentucky. The website contains information on the influence of Kentucky on Lincoln's beliefs and actions, a list of events, information about Lincoln sites to visit, educational resources, and information about grants.

Mr. Lincoln's Virtual Library
The Library of Congress
http://memory.loc.gov/ammem/alhtml/alhome.html

> This site catalogs 30,000 documents relating to Mr. Lincoln's life and times, including correspondence, personal papers, books, pamphlets, broadsides, prints, cartoons, maps, drawings, photos and more. It's fairly easy to find what you want (e.g., a handwritten copy of the Gettysburg Address or the Emancipation Proclamation, a poster offering a reward for the capture of John Wilkes Booth, sheet music for campaign songs).

The Time of the Lincolns
www.pbs.org/wgbh/amex/lincolns

> Put Abraham Lincoln in context in this terrific site for teachers and older students. It's based on the documentary "Abraham and Mary Lincoln: A House Divided" from PBS, but stands quite well on its own. Includes lots of primary source material, an interactive map, videos, articles on the culture, politics and economy of the U.S. in the 19th Century.

4. OTHER USEFUL STUFF

Some fascinating materials and projects are out there. Here are a few that are available for school use.

Traveling Trunks

Trunks full of primary source documents and artifacts are available from the Lincoln Boyhood National Memorial and the Abraham Lincoln Birthplace National Historic site, both of which are operated by the National Park Service. The trunk itself weighs 38 pounds; it is about three feet long and a foot and a half high. A sample inventory includes reproduction of 19th Century clothing, a slate and slate pencil, a set of wood carders, a period game, period books (e.g., *Aesop's Fables*), reproductions of primary source documents (e.g., Gettysburg Address, Emancipation Proclamation), video tapes, curriculum guides, photographs, activity cards and more.

Trunks are lent to schools for one week – though longer periods can be arranged. There is no cost to the school, except for shipping. (The Lincoln Boyhood Home pays the costs of shipping one way.) To make a reservation contact the site:

Abraham Lincoln Birthplace National Historic Site
2995 Lincoln Farm Road
Hodgenville, KY 42748
270-358-3137
www.nps.gov/abli/forteachers/travellingtrunks.htm

Lincoln Boyhood National Memorial
2916 E South Street
Lincoln City, IN 47552
(812) 937-4541
www.nps.gov/libo/forteachers/travellingtrunks.htm

The HistoryMobile

The Kentucky Historical Society's HistoryMobile is a traveling exhibit housed in a 45-foot semi-trailer. The exhibit tells the story of Mr. Lincoln's childhood in Kentucky, his journey from log cabin to lawyering, his struggle to end slavery, and his dealings with Kentucky during the Civil War through audio, video, artifacts and images.

HistoryMobile season runs April-October; schools must reserve several months in advance. There is no charge for the HistoryMobile but sponsoring organizations are asked to pay for or provide lodging for the program coordinator. For more information or to schedule a HistoryMobile visit, contact David Whealdon at david.whealdon@ky.gov or 502-226-0802.

Artifacts and Documents
www.histdocs.com

Purchase replicas of Lincoln's important speeches (as they were published in his time) from the Historical Documents Company. Campaign posters, quill pens, Confederate money and other reproductions are also available.

Kentucky Lincoln Heritage Trail Passport Program
www.kylincolntrail.com/trailMap.aspx

Share this with parents who'd like to learn more about Mr. Lincoln along with their children. They can pick up a passport for their child at any of the sites on Kentucky's Lincoln Heritage Trail. Whenever they visit each Lincoln site, their passports are stamped to indicate their visit. With ten stamps, the child's name is entered into a prize drawing. See interactive map at www.kylincolntrail.com.

Kentucky Chautauqua Program
Kentucky Humanities Council
www.kyhumanities.org/forschools.html

Bring a character from Mr. Lincoln's past to interact with your students: perhaps Mr. Lincoln himself, his sister-in-law Emilie Todd, or a slave who worked for Ms. Todd's family. Kentucky Chautauqua programs are one-person dramas lasting about 45 minutes. The Humanities Council asks that audiences include at least 40 students. Cost is $150 for the first program, but you can ask about "one-site" fees for additional programs presented at the same location.

5. LESSON PLANS

Many Lincoln-related lessons are available online. Here are a few that are notable.

Abraham Lincoln Bicentennial Commission
www.kylincoln.org/education

Teachers involved in the teacher network of Kentucky's Abraham Lincoln Bicentennial Commission have been working on a series of lesson plans about Abraham Lincoln and support materials. They are intended to be an integral part of the curriculum, not an addition to it. Lessons are posted on the Kentucky Lincoln Bicentennial website. The lessons include resources and support materials. While Mr. Lincoln's Kentucky connections are included, they are not the focus of the lessons.

Essential questions for the series of lessons are as follows:

Primary
- *Why* and *how* do we remember individuals who are part of our history?

Fourth Grade
- How did Lincoln's ties to Kentucky and Indiana shape him as a person and a leader?
- Why were Illinois, Kentucky and Indiana important to Abraham Lincoln during his presidency?

Fifth Grade
- How did significant events in Abraham Lincoln's lifetime shape his beliefs, values and actions as a leader in the U.S.?
- Why has Abraham Lincoln remained a significant historical figure?

Eighth Grade
- How did sectional differences between the North and South influence the election of 1860?
- How did groups in the North, South and West react to Abraham Lincoln's political beliefs in the election of 1860?
- How did events following the election of 1860 force the newly-elected President Lincoln to demonstrate his leadership abilities in a time of crisis?
- How did President Lincoln use his leadership skills to unify a divided nation?

High School
- How did Abraham Lincoln's views on Reconstruction affect the policies of his successors and the American government?
- How are basic principles of government changed and affected by a time of national crisis?

Lesson Plans Developed by the National Park Service
www.nps.gov/abli/forteachers/curriculummaterials.htm

Thirty teachers from Illinois, Indiana and Kentucky worked with the National Park Service to develop four excellent lessons emphasizing how the challenges of frontier life shaped Mr. Lincoln's fundamental character, giving him the resolve and leadership needed to lead the nation successfully through the Civil War. Lessons include essential questions, key concepts/skills, curriculum standards, procedures, activities, preparation of materials and resources, background information for teachers, and products/assessment, including writing prompts. All materials, including sing-a-longs and video clips, are available on this site.

Grades 3-5: Abraham Lincoln — Great Learner/Great Leader

Students will investigate the life of Mr. Lincoln by participating in an agree/disagree activity, listening to stories related by the teacher, viewing a musical slide show, reading secondary and primary sources, analyzing information, and communicating their learning by responding orally and in writing.

Grades 6-8: Lincoln's Views on Slavery

Students will look briefly at how Mr. Lincoln's views on slavery might have been influenced by his parents and others throughout his life. They will understand that there were varying views of slavery in the mid-19th Century.

Grades 6-8: Abraham Lincoln's Kentucky Influences

Many people influenced Mr. Lincoln's life and way of thinking. Students create a product (brochure, PowerPoint presentation, video, etc.) that gives their readers/viewers insight into the connections Mr. Lincoln had with his roots.

Grades 5-12: Women on the American Frontier

Participants will learn about the contributions women made to life on the frontier as revealed through various women with whom Mr. Lincoln came in contact. They will be able to explain how the role of women on the frontier was not only an effect of traditional gender roles but of necessity.

Lincoln/Net
http://lincoln.lib.niu.edu/teachers/lessons.html

Lincoln/Net offers teachers lesson plans that utilize the primary documents found in the Lincoln/Net database. Primary documents and images relating to Lincoln's experiences in Springfield and New Salem provide background to places that shaped Lincoln's political career. The website also includes interactive maps, multimedia slideshows, video and audio files, and more useful supplements for instruction.

6. DOCUMENTS

IN LINCOLN'S WORDS

Emancipation Proclamation
January 1, 1863

Following the preliminary Emancipation Proclamation of September 22, 1862, Lincoln's Proclamation of January 1, 1863, formally emancipates all slaves held in states or parts of states in active rebellion against the Union.

By the President of the United States of America:
A Proclamation.

Whereas, on the twenty-second day of September, in the year of our Lord one thousand eight hundred and sixty-two, a proclamation was issued by the President of the United States, containing, among other things, the following, to wit:

That on the first day of January, in the year of our Lord one thousand eight hundred and sixty-three, all persons held as slaves within any State or designated part of a State, the people whereof shall then be in rebellion against the United States, shall be then, thenceforward, and forever free; and the Executive Government of the United States, including the military and naval authority thereof, will recognize and maintain the freedom of such persons, and will do no act or acts to repress such persons, or any of them, in any efforts they may make for their actual freedom.

That the Executive will, on the first day of January aforesaid, by proclamation, designate the States and parts of States, if any, in which the people thereof, respectively, shall then be in rebellion against the United States; and the fact that any State, or the people thereof, shall on that day be, in good faith, represented in the Congress of the United States by members chosen thereto at elections wherein a majority of the qualified voters of such State shall have participated, shall, in the absence of strong countervailing testimony, be deemed conclusive evidence that such State, and the people thereof, are not then in rebellion against the United States.

Now, therefore I, Abraham Lincoln, President of the United States, by virtue of the power in me vested as Commander-in-Chief of the Army and Navy of the United States in time of actual armed rebellion against the authority and government of the United States, and as a fit and necessary war measure for suppressing said rebellion, do, on this first day of January, in the year of our Lord one thousand eight hundred and sixty-three, and in accordance with my purpose so to do publicly proclaim for the full period of one hundred days, from the day first above mentioned, order and designate as the States and parts of States wherein the people thereof respectively, are this day in rebellion against the United States, the following, to wit:

Arkansas, Texas, Louisiana (except the Parishes of St. Bernard, Plaquemines, Jefferson, St.

John, St. Charles, St. James Ascension, Assumption, Terrebonne, Lafourche, St. Mary, St. Martin, and Orleans, including the City of New Orleans)[,] Mississippi, Alabama, Florida, Georgia, South Carolina, North Carolina, and Virginia, (except the forty-eight counties designated as West Virginia, and also the counties of Berkley, Accomac, Northampton, Elizabeth City, York, Princess Ann, and Norfolk, including the cities of Norfolk and Portsmouth), and which excepted parts, are for the present, left precisely as if this proclamation were not issued.

And by virtue of the power, and for the purpose aforesaid, I do order and declare that all persons held as slaves within said designated States, and parts of States, are, and henceforward shall be free; and that the Executive government of the United States, including the military and naval authorities thereof, will recognize and maintain the freedom of said persons.

And I hereby enjoin upon the people so declared to be free to abstain from all violence, unless in necessary self-defence; and I recommend to them that, in all cases when allowed, they labor faithfully for reasonable wages.

And I further declare and make known, that such persons of suitable condition, will be received into the armed service of the United States to garrison forts, positions, stations, and other places, and to man vessels of all sorts in said service.

And upon this act, sincerely believed to be an act of justice, warranted by the Constitution, upon military necessity, I invoke the considerate judgment of mankind, and the gracious favor of Almighty God.

In witness whereof, I have hereunto set my hand and caused the seal of the United States to be affixed.

Done at the City of Washington, this first day of January, in the year of our Lord one thousand eight hundred and sixty three, and of the Independence of the United States of America the eighty-seventh.

By the President: ABRAHAM LINCOLN
WILLIAM H. SEWARD, Secretary of State

IN LINCOLN'S WORDS

Gettysburg Address
November 19, 1863

Four months after the Battle of Gettysburg, Lincoln joined in a dedication of a national cemetery on a portion of the battlefield. The speech he delivered that day would become one of the most famous speeches given by a U.S. President.

Four score and seven years ago our fathers brought forth on this continent, a new nation, conceived in Liberty, and dedicated to the proposition that all men are created equal.

Now we are engaged in a great civil war, testing whether that nation, or any nation so conceived and so dedicated, can long endure. We are met on a great battlefield of that war. We have come to dedicate a portion of that field, as a final resting place for those who here gave their lives that that nation might live. It is altogether fitting and proper that we should do this.

But, in a larger sense, we can not dedicate — we can not consecrate — we can not hallow this ground. The brave men, living and dead, who struggled here, have consecrated it, far above our poor power to add or detract. The world will little note, nor long remember what we say here, but it can never forget what they did here. It is for us the living, rather, to be dedicated here to the unfinished work which they who fought here have thus far so nobly advanced. It is rather for us to be here dedicated to the great task remaining before us — that from these honored dead we take increased devotion to that cause for which they gave the last full measure of devotion — that we here highly resolve that these dead shall not have died in vain; that this nation, under God, shall have a new birth of freedom; and that government of the people, by the people, for the people, shall not perish from the earth.

IN LINCOLN'S WORDS

Letter to Grace Bedell

When Mr. Lincoln was a candidate for President, he received quite a bit of fan mail. One letter was from 11-year-old Grace Bedell who had an idea how he could win the election.

October 15, 1860

Dear Sir:

My father has just home from the fair and brought home your picture and Mr. Hamlin's. I am a little girl only 11 years old, but want you should be President of the United States very much so I hope you wont think me very bold to write to such a great man as you are. Have you any little girls about as large as I am if so give them my love and tell her to write to me if you cannot answer this letter. I have got 4 brother's and part of them will vote for you any way and if you let your whiskers grow I will try and get the rest of them to vote for you you would look a great deal better for your face is so thin. All the ladies like whiskers and they would tease their husband's to vote for you and then you would be President. My father is going to vote for you and if I was a man I would vote for you to but I will try to get every one to vote for you that I can I think that rail fence around your picture makes it look very pretty I have got a little baby sister she is nine weeks old and is just as cunning as can be. When you direct your letter direct to Grace Bedell Westfield Chatauque County New York. I must not write any more answer this letter right off. Good bye.

Grace Bedell

Mr. Lincoln's response:

My dear little Miss.

Your very agreeable letter of the 15th is received – I regret the necessity of saying I have no daughters – I have three sons – one seventeen, one nine, and one seven years of age – They, with their mother, constitute my whole family – As to the whiskers, having never worn any, do you not think people would call it a piece of silly affection if I were to begin it now?

Your very sincere well wisher

A. Lincoln

[NOTE: Mr. Lincoln grew the beard. And he won the election.]

IN LINCOLN'S WORDS

Second Inaugural Address
March 04, 1865

Just over a month before his assassination, Lincoln gives his brief yet poignant second Inaugural Address. With the end of the Civil War rapidly approaching, Lincoln uses the opportunity to look toward the eventual peace and reconstruction of the Union. Note that he begins his closing remarks with the famous words "With malice toward none; with charity for all."

Fellow-Countrymen:

At this second appearing to take the oath of the Presidential office there is less occasion for an extended address than there was at the first. Then a statement somewhat in detail of a course to be pursued seemed fitting and proper. Now, at the expiration of four years, during which public declarations have been constantly called forth on every point and phase of the great contest which still absorbs the attention and engrosses the energies of the nation, little that is new could be presented. The progress of our arms, upon which all else chiefly depends, is as well known to the public as to myself, and it is, I trust, reasonably satisfactory and encouraging to all. With high hope for the future, no prediction in regard to it is ventured.

On the occasion corresponding to this four years ago all thoughts were anxiously directed to an impending civil war. All dreaded it, all sought to avert it. While the inaugural address was being delivered from this place, devoted altogether to saving the Union without war, insurgent agents were in the city seeking to destroy it without war – seeking to dissolve the Union and divide effects by negotiation. Both parties deprecated war, but one of them would make war rather than let the nation survive, and the other would accept war rather than let it perish, and the war came.

One-eighth of the whole population were colored slaves, not distributed generally over the Union. but localized in the southern part of it. These slaves constituted a peculiar and powerful interest. All knew that this interest was somehow the cause of the war. To strengthen, perpetuate, and extend this interest was the object for which the insurgents would rend the Union even by war, while the Government claimed no right to do more than to restrict the territorial enlargement of it. Neither party expected for the war the magnitude or the duration which it has already attained. Neither anticipated that the cause of the conflict might cease with or even before the conflict itself should cease. Each looked for an easier triumph, and a result less fundamental and astounding. Both read the same Bible and pray to the same God, and each invokes His aid against the other. It may seem strange that any men should dare to ask a just God's assistance in wringing their bread from the sweat of other men's faces, but let us judge not, that we be not judged. The prayers of both could not be answered. That of neither has been answered fully. The Almighty has His own purposes. "Woe unto the world because of offenses; for it must needs be that offenses come, but woe to that man by whom the offense cometh." If we shall suppose that American slavery is one of those offenses which, in the providence of God, must needs come, but which, having continued through His appointed time, He now wills to remove, and that He gives to both North and South this terrible war as the woe due to those by whom the offense came, shall we discern therein any departure from those divine attributes which the believers in a living God always ascribe to Him? Fondly do we hope, fervently do we pray, that this mighty scourge of war may speedily pass away. Yet, if God wills that it continue until all the wealth piled by the bondsman's two hundred and fifty years of unrequited toil shall be sunk, and until every drop of blood drawn with the lash shall be paid by another drawn with the sword, as was said three thousand years ago, so still it must be said "the judgments of the Lord are true and righteous altogether."

With malice toward none, with charity for all, with firmness in the right as God gives us to see the right, let us strive on to finish the work we are in, to bind up the nation's wounds, to care for him who shall have borne the battle and for his widow and his orphan, to do all which may achieve and cherish a just and lasting peace among ourselves and with all nations.

IN LINCOLN'S WORDS

"Not Much of Me"
An autobiography written by Abraham Lincoln in 1859

I was born Feb. 12, 1809, in Hardin County, Kentucky. My parents were both born in Virginia, of undistinguished families – second families, perhaps I should say. My mother, who died in my tenth year, was of a family of the name of Hanks, some of whom now reside in Adams and others in Macon counties, Illinois. My paternal grandfather, Abraham Lincoln, emigrated from Rockingham County, Virginia, to Kentucky, about 1781 or 2, where, a year or two later, he was killed by Indians, not in battle, but by stealth, when he was laboring to open a farm in the forest. His ancestors, who were Quakers, went to Virginia from Berks County, Pennsylvania. An effort to identify them with the New-England family of the same name ended in nothing more definite than a similarity of Christian names in both families, such as Enoch, Levi, Mordecai, Solomon, Abraham, and the like.

My father, at the death of his father, was but six years of age; and he grew up, litterally without education. He removed from Kentucky to what is now Spencer county, Indiana, in my eighth year. We reached our new home about the time the State came in the Union. It was a wild region, with many bears and other wild animals still in the woods. There I grew up. There were some schools, so called; but no qualification was ever required of a teacher, beyond "readin, writin, and cipherin," to the Rule of Three. If a straggler supposed to understand latin, happened to sojourn in the neighborhood, he was looked upon as a wizzard. There was absolutely nothing to excite ambition for education. Of course when I came of age I did not know much. Still somehow, I could read, write, and cipher to the Rule of Three; but that was all. I have not been to school since. The little advance I now have upon this store of education, I have picked up from time to time under the pressure of necessity.

I was raised to farm work, which I continued till I was twenty-two. At twenty-one I came to Illinois, and passed the first year in Illinois – Macon county. Then I got to New-Salem, (at that time in Sangamon, now in Menard county), where I remained a year as a sort of Clerk in a store. Then came the Black-Hawk war; and I was elected a Captain of Volunteers – a success which gave me more pleasure than any I have had since. I went the campaign, was elated, ran for the Legislature the same year (1832) and was beaten – the only time I have been beaten by the people. The next, and three succeeding biennial elections, I was elected to the Legislature. I was not a candidate afterwards. During this Legislative period I had studied law, and removed to Springfield to practice it. In 1846 I was once elected to the lower House of Congress. Was not a candidate for re-election. From 1849 to 1854, both inclusive, practiced law more assiduously than ever before. Always a Whig in politics, and generally on the Whig electoral tickets, making active canvasses. I was losing interest in politics, when the repeal of the Missouri Compromise aroused me again. What I have done since then is pretty well known.

If any personal description of me is thought desirable, it may be said, I am, in height, six feet, four inches, nearly; lean in flesh, weighing, on an average, one hundred and eighty pounds; dark complexion, with coarse black hair, and grey eyes – no other marks or brands recollected.

A LINCOLN MEMORIAL

An Editorial in The New York Times
January 13, 1907
by Mark Twain

Mark Twain wrote this in connection with the effort to make the Lincoln Birthplace a national park.

There is a natural human instinct that is gratified by the sight of anything hallowed by association with a great man or with great deeds. So many people make pilgrimages to the town whose streets were once trodden by Shakespeare, and Hartford guarded her Charter Oak for centuries because it had once had a hole in it that helped to save the liberties of a Colony. But in most cases the connection between the great man or the great event and the relic we revere is accidental. Shakespeare might have lived in any other town as well as in Stratford, and Connecticut's charter might have been hidden in a woodchuck hole as well as in the Charter Oak. But it was no accident that planted Lincoln on a Kentucky farm, halfway between the Lakes and the Gulf. The association there had substance in it. Lincoln belonged just where he was put. If the Union wanted to be saved, it had to be a man of such an origin that should save it. No wintry New England Brahmin could have done it, or any torrid cotton-planter, regarding the distant Yankee as a species of obnoxious foreigner. It needed a man of the Border, where Civil War meant the grapple of brother with brother and disunion a raw and gaping wound. It needed one who knew slavery not from books only, but as a living thing, knew the good that was mixed with its evil, and knew the evil, not merely as it affected the negroes, but in its hardly less baleful influence upon the whites. It needed one who knew how human all the parties to the quarrel were, how much alike they were at bottom, who saw them all reflected in himself, and felt their dissensions like the tearing apart of his own soul. When the war came, Georgia sent an army in gray and Massachusetts an army in blue, but Kentucky raised armies for both sides. And this man, sprung from Southern poor whites, born on a Kentucky farm, transplanted to an Illinois village, this man, in whose heart knowledge and charity had left no room for malice, was marked by Providence as the one to 'bind up the nation's wounds.'

7. IMAGES

These bas relief panels are installed at the Lincoln Boyhood National Memorial in Indiana.

Kentucky panel

Indiana panel

Illinois panel

Washington panel

'He Belongs To The Ages' panel

Lincoln's humble childhood was spent in two states, both of which he claimed as positive influences.

Lincoln Birthplace - Kentucky

Nancy Hanks Lincoln
(the President's mother)

Lincoln Boyhood Home - Indiana

Thomas Lincoln
(the President's father)

This house in Springfield, Illinois, is the only home Abraham and Mary Lincoln ever owned. When they bought it, it was a one-and-a-half story cottage, but they expanded it to two full stories.

Shown here are three portraits of Abraham and Mary Todd Lincoln and their family. Notice the similarities (and differences) in the two images of Lincoln and his son reading.

In a period well before radio, television, recording, or the Internet, political campaigns relied almost entirely on live speeches, newspaper or magazine articles, slogan buttons, and posters such as these.

Lincoln's inaugurations were documented by photographers and sketch artists whose images, in time, were shared throughout the nation and around the world.

*Lincoln's presidency was largely defined by
the Emancipation Proclamation
(its drafting is portrayed in the image above)
and by the U.S. Civil War, 1861-1865.*

Presidential assassinations are rare in American history. Not surprisingly, the nation, although in mourning, was captivated by the biggest news story of 1865 – Lincoln's sudden death and the people who were responsible for it.

This statue stands at the entrance of the Lincoln Memorial University campus.
Cumberland Gap is in the background.